Journeying with Jonah

the struggle to find yourself

Journeying with Jonah

the struggle to find yourself

Denis McBride C.Ss.R.

redemptorist
publications

Published by **Redemptorist Publications**
Alphonsus House, Chawton, Hampshire, GU34 3HQ, UK
Tel. +44 (0)1420 88222, Fax. +44 (0)1420 88805
Email: rp@rpbooks.co.uk, www.rpbooks.co.uk

A registered charity limited by guarantee
Registered in England 3261721

Copyright © Denis McBride, 2015
First published October 2015

Edited by Bahram Francis Rafat
Designed by Eliana Thompson
Cover and internal illustrations by Jonathan Thompson

ISBN: 978-0-85231-438-8

A CIP catalogue record for this book is available from the British Library.

The publisher gratefully acknowledges permission to use the following copyright material:
Cover and internal illustrations by Jonathan Thompson: © Jonathan Thompson @ Meadow Press, www.jonathan-thompson.com
P20: © 2015 J. Nelson Kraybill, www.peace-pilgrim.com.
P39-41: Painting of Isaiah, Jeremiah and Ezekiel (1512) Michelangelo, Sistine Chapel ceiling.
P106: Photograph by Poulpy via Wikimedia Commons.
P7: Extract from *A Masque of Mercy* from The Poetry of Robert Frost by Robert Frost, published by Jonathan Cape. Reprinted by permission of The Random House Group Limited.
Excerpts from the New Revised Standard Version Bible: Anglicised Edition, © 1989, 1995, National Council of the Churches of Christ in the United States of America. Used by permission. All rights reserved.

The Book of Jonah is from the New Revised Standard Version of the Bible, copyright © 1989 National Council of the Churches of Christ in the USA. Used by permission. All rights reserved.

Psalms from the Grail Psalter reprinted by permission of HarperCollins Publishers Ltd © 1963.

The publisher has made all reasonable effort to trace copyright holders and any omissions will be corrected at reprint.

Printed by Lithgo Press Ltd.,
Leicester LE8 6NU

For
my sister Ellen
the good-hearted
matriarch of our family

By the same author

The Gospel of Luke
The Gospel of Mark
Emmaus: the Gracious Visit of God
Jesus and the Gospels
Where does the Jesus Story Begin?
Impressions of Jesus
The Parables of Jesus
Praying with Pictures
Waiting on God (also e-book)
Journeying with Jesus: a Companion's Guide
Journeying with Jesus: a Guide for Groups
Journeying towards Jesus in Advent
Borrowing the Eyes of Others: Paintings Vol 1
Awakening to Yourself: Paintings Vol 2
Seasons of the Word: Reflections on the Sunday Readings
Diary for the Year of Faith
Diary for the Year of Matthew
Diary for the Year of Mark
Praying the Rosary – a Journey through Scripture and Art (also e-book)
Diary for the Year of Mercy

Electronic

Jesus and the Gospels: 36 lectures on CD
Reflecting on Paintings: 10 reflections on CD
Where Does the Jesus Story Begin? 10 lectures on CD
Seasons of the Word: Complete reflections on CD

The Gospel of John (DVD)
The Power of the Parables (DVD)
The Passion of Jesus (DVD)
The Transfiguration in the Gospel and in life (DVD)

www.denismcbride.com

You should be an authority on Mercy.
That book of yours in the Old Testament
Is the first place in literature, I think,
Where Mercy is explicitly the subject.
I say you should be proud of having beaten
The Gospels to it.

Paul speaks to the prophet Jonah
in Robert Frost's verse-drama, *A Masque of Mercy*

They say, Find a purpose in your life and live it.
But, sometimes, it is only after you have lived
that you recognize your life had a purpose, and
likely one you never had in mind.

Khaled Hosseini,
And the Mountains Echoed

Contents

Introduction..11

PART ONE – THE FIRST MISSION...17

The call
Jonah and Jesus
The mission
The great city of Nineveh
Crossing boundaries
Identity, direction, outlook
Jonah goes down
Why does Jonah flee?
From Major to Minor

PART TWO – ALL AT SEA....................45

The storm
The response of the sailors
The sleep of Jonah
The captain intervenes
Casting of lots
The sailors question Jonah
Jonah's cautious response
Jonah's penance
The sailors' prayer
Prophet overboard

PART THREE – IN THE DEEP..............75

The great fish
Prayer: Jonah reflects on the past
Prayer: Jonah describes his situation
Prayer: Jonah remembers the Lord
Prayer: Jonah makes his promises
Back on dry land

PART FOUR –
THE SECOND MISSION

PART FOUR –
THE SECOND MISSION......................99

The prophet is called again
Jonah responds to God's call
Nineveh's change of heart
The decree and hope of the king
God's response

PART FIVE –
THE UNFINISHED ENDING..............119

The angry response of Jonah
Jonah's death wish
Jonah sulks and waits
The withered tree
God's final challenge

Conclusion...................................142
God's indiscriminate mercy

Appendix.....................................146
The Book of Jonah
(New Revised Standard Version)

Introduction

Personally I think that the prophet Jonah is a sympathetic partner, albeit a curious one, to help us review our lives. Although a believer in God, Jonah struggles to come to terms with the awful strangeness of God's choices which do not mirror his own; he grapples to find his true self and purpose in life; he tries to flee from the presence of God, hoping to find a sanctuary for himself beyond God's reach; he is angry when he finds that God is not angry but all-merciful.

Jonah is not numbered among the Major Prophets – like Isaiah or Jeremiah or Ezekiel – but is placed in the second division among the twelve Minor Prophets, a subordinate to the greats who are celebrated for their commitment, revered for their fidelity to the word of God, honoured for their unwavering courage in the face of opposition. They are intellectual giants, giving memorable and lengthy speeches; Jonah, by contrast, utters one line. As Major Prophets they speak with authority across the ages: clearly they have earned their place in the primary canon as single-minded and persistent servants of God.

Unlike all the other prophetic books, the book of Jonah is about the character of the prophet rather than the content of his message: we are invited to follow his story, not attend his discourses. His tale is alive with ambiguity and doubt: it is stunningly modern. Neither single-minded nor persistent, Jonah appears as someone who has emerged from among us: someone who has to struggle to find himself, someone who has yet to grow into his true identity, someone who has to discover his direction in life, someone who has to allow his own outlook on life to be shaped by God's mercy.

Although a prophet, he seems forever hesitant about what is expected of him. Jonah is temperamental; he seems always in transition, never at home anywhere, unsure of what to do, floundering, hesitating, forever worried about his reputation in the eyes of others. He refuses to go where he is supposed to go. Commanded by God to go north-east by land, he decides to go due west by sea. He is the patron saint of everyone who has been appointed to impossible places.

When you watch him, you might wonder if you are in a theatre watching a desperate actor stumbling around a vast stage, looking for a compass to find an exit.

Personally, I feel at ease in his troubled company. How can you not like this minor prophet? I do, not least because at the beginning of the last century, the Redemptorists in London were known as "the poor man's Jesuit". And when I gave a retreat to the Kiltegan priests in Ireland, they told me that they were called "Jesuits in wellingtons". Clearly, the Jesuits were heading up the major league – they certainly are now, with the first Jesuit pope. It appears that the Redemptorists and the Kiltegans are still relegated to the second division.

Maybe this is why I love Jonah.

I think that this minor-league prophet mirrors so much of who we are: flawed, fearful, restless, driven. Jonah is opinionated and not shy to express his thinking, even to God. Over against what God commands, Jonah, a real modern, consults himself and travels on his own instincts. Being true to what he believes or fears is more important to him than being obedient to God. He sees God as a contestant, not a supreme guide or even an ally, and so he argues, weighing up the options and deciding to follow his own way.

One of the most thoughtful responses to the book of Jonah is Herman Melville's *Moby Dick*. The chaplain to the sailors, Father Mapple, preaching on Jonah, summarises the core challenge:

> As with all sinners among men, the sin of this son of Amittai was in his wilful disobedience of the command of God – never mind now what that command was, or how conveyed – which he found a hard command. But all the things that God would have us do are hard for us to do – remember that – and hence, he oftener commands us than endeavours to persuade. And if we obey God, we must disobey ourselves, wherein the hardness of obeying God consists.[1]

In obeying himself Jonah disobeys God. His story then becomes one of suspense: he almost succeeds in escaping; the ship almost breaks up; Jonah almost dies by drowning; Nineveh is almost destroyed; the tree that gives Jonah shade almost survives. In this story we are on the edge of things.

There is one constant in the book of Jonah: Jonah's belief that God's indiscriminate mercy extended to the pagans of Nineveh is not only inappropriate but incomprehensible: Jonah is scandalised by God's mercy. Our minor prophet has to learn as we all do, that mercy is indivisible: we cannot plead for mercy for ourselves and then deny it to others.

---

[1] Herman Melville, *Moby Dick* (Oxford: Oxford University Press, 1998), 37.

What missionary, proclaiming God's message, nurses not the hope but the fear that the people will repent and enjoy God's mercy? In *Misericodiae Vultus* (The Face of Mercy), in which Pope Francis proclaims the Jubilee Year of Mercy, he writes:

> When faced with the gravity of sin, God responds with the fullness of mercy. Mercy will always be greater than any sin, and no one can place limits on the love of God who is ever ready to forgive. (*Misericordiae Vultus*, 3)

The book of Jonah explores the prophet's struggle to place limits on the mercy of God. But this book proclaims good news about God: God's mercy is a powerful force that keeps the future open; tender-heartedness breaks the chain of determinism, seeing the time ahead as a graced place for change. No one, but no one, is beyond the reach of God's mercy; no one is locked into a planned fate; no one is doomed to embrace disaster. The book of Jonah heralds the Gospel and the merciful message of Jesus.

Further, there is Jonah's attendant fear that if God is indeed merciful, then he, his messenger, will be considered a fool after his fatal pronouncement about the sure destruction of the city. Thus our reluctant prophet is worried about his persona, his reputation and how others might judge his performance. Anxious about his celebrity status, he wants to be right and be proved to be right.

Jonah yearns for affirmation of his own way of seeing things: without that approval he will try to flee to the ends of the earth, to hide from the presence of God – he should have learned from Adam's failure. As Elie Wiesel has written:

> Jonah's book is so well written that one is not surprised by his lack of success. Unhappy, unlucky always. Rarely does anything good happen to him. No honours, no rewards, no friends, no supporters. Whatever he undertakes seems to go wrong. Whenever he wishes to win, he loses; whenever he would prefer to lose, he wins. He is a displaced person, living in an internal exile.[2]

By the end of the book of Jonah our incomplete hero is still in internal exile: he has not yet arrived at his true self; his direction remains unclear and his outlook unformed by the will of God. Jonah's story concludes as he is cross-examined by a God who is as stubbornly patient and merciful to Jonah as he was to the people of Nineveh. His story ends with a question. God's question about his right to be merciful hovers over the story; we do not hear Jonah's answer. We have to find our own.

---

[2] Elie Wiesel, *Five Biblical Portraits* (Indiana: University of Notre Dame Press, 2005), 135.

The first mission

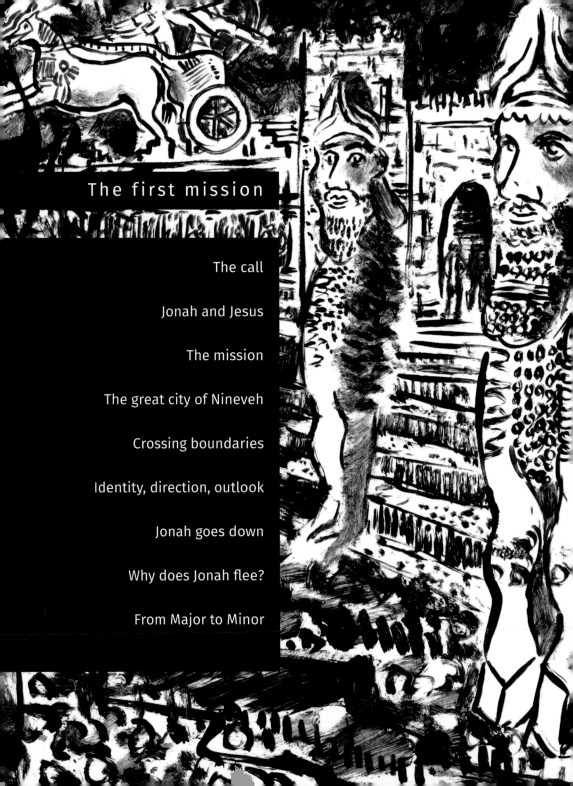

The first mission

The call

Jonah and Jesus

The mission

The great city of Nineveh

Crossing boundaries

Identity, direction, outlook

Jonah goes down

Why does Jonah flee?

From Major to Minor

The call

Now the word of the LORD came to Jonah son of Amittai, saying, "Go at once to Nineveh, that great city, and cry out against it; for their wickedness has come up before me." (Jonah 1:1)

The divine word is first, precipitating the story; this divine command will drive and shape the whole narrative. As the book of Jonah opens with the word of the Lord addressed directly to the prophet, so it will close in the same way. Without the word of the Lord there would be no story, no dilemma, no flight, no rescue, no repentance and no final challenge. We are not told how the word of the Lord comes to Jonah, whether in dream or vision, only that it comes from outside Jonah. This word, unwelcomed by Jonah, comes *in medias res*, in the middle of things, and will set the stage for the drama. What has happened before this word was spoken is left unsaid.

The call to Jonah is not an invitation to be considered but a command to be followed. Our protagonist is called Jonah, son of Amittai - Jonah's name is the Hebrew word for dove and his family name means the Lord is faithful. If the dove is a sign of peace and new beginnings, Jonah will become, in spite of himself, a sign of peace and new beginnings for the sailors at sea and for the people of Nineveh; but not, sadly, for himself.

The story begins with a life interrupted: a typical biblical beginning. We are not offered a leisurely introduction to our hero, informed of his background, his family and personal circumstances; we are neither notified of his virtues nor alerted to his compulsions. Like Mary and Joseph in the New Testament, we meet Jonah for the first time when his life is interrupted by a new challenge. And like Mary and Joseph, his character will be revealed through how he faces this new summons.

If all stories proceed through conflict – there is no story without one – then writers usually establish the conflict early in the story. "Once upon a time everyone lived happily ever after" is not a story for the simple reason that it contains no conflict. Conflict involves friction, tension and struggle – the driving force of story. If there is nothing in a story to fight against, nothing to win, nothing to lose, why would anyone bother reading on? If the principal character never struggles, is never tested by adversity, never battles either against forces outside or within, the story goes nowhere. It is essential to the drama that there is nothing automatic about success.

Conflict is not just essential to the development of a story – it is the essence of every story. What makes a story interesting and engaging is the conflict that stands between the hero and his goal. Readers want to become involved in the hero's personal battle to achieve the specified goal, and if the writer successfully engages the readers in that struggle they will worry: will the hero manage to reach his goal or will he become disturbed and fearful by the challenges he faces, settling for avoidance? Conflict stimulates that worry.

It is clear from the first verse that Jonah's opinion is not sought; rather, he is commanded by the divine imperative, "Go... cry out..." He is given no time to prepare for this demanding mission; his immediate obedience is assumed. How will Jonah respond to the outer voice that commands him where to go and what to do? Will he answer by saying "Yes, thy will be done" or will the new challenge prove too much for him? Or will he follow his inner voice that tells him where to go and what to do?

Jonah and Jesus

Jonah's name appears in 2 Kings 14:25 identifying a prophet who came from Gath-hepher, a town situated in Lower Galilee, about three miles north-east of Nazareth. All that remains of that ancient town is a large mound (see above). Jonah and Jesus were not only countrymen, but came from the same neighbourhood in Lower Galilee. Surely, in growing up, Jesus would have heard of the exploits of his famous neighbour from up the road. Certainly, Jonah is the only prophet that Jesus ever compares himself to:

For just as Jonah was three days and three nights in the belly of the sea monster, so for three days and three nights the Son of Man will be in the heart of the earth. The people of Nineveh will rise up at the judgement with this generation and condemn it, because they repented at the proclamation of Jonah, and see, something greater than Jonah is here!

(Matthew 12:40-41)

Jesus celebrates the success of Jonah's mission to Nineveh, arguing that the Ninevites will become the accusers of those who hear Jesus but do not attend his words. As Philip Cary writes:

Jesus is the sign of Jonah because he is a sign the same way Jonah is a sign. Jonah offered Nineveh no sign but himself. He did no miracles and had little to say, and that little was ironic and enigmatic, like a parable about not knowing what time it is. The mystery, the hidden meaning, is right there on the surface, as if to say: Don't you know whose word you're hearing? That's what time it is, the time when your Lord visits you and speaks to you. And *now* you want a sign? The Ninevites knew better, and when Jonah came as a sign among them they believed his word and repented.[3]

---

[3] Phillip Carey, *Jonah*, SCM Theological Commentary on the Bible (London: SCM Press, 2008), 80-81.

The mission

Jonah is commanded to go to Nineveh, the great capital of Assyria, which was built on the banks of the River Tigris in north-eastern Mesopotamia, now Iraq. The northern kingdom of Israel had been destroyed by Assyria (see 2 Kings 17) in 721 BC and its tribes disappeared from history; they are sometimes referred to as "the ten lost tribes" in extra-biblical literature. Assyria was at the height of its power between the eighth and seven centuries BC and was feared throughout the ancient Near East for its imperialistic ambition and its brutality, uprooting whole peoples and leaving a wasteland in its wake.

Now the Israelite Jonah is being sent to the destroyer's capital city to offer the inhabitants the opportunity of repentance. Jonah is the only prophet of Israel sent on a personal mission to the Gentiles: where other prophets railed against the nations from the safety of their home territory, Jonah is commanded to make a personal appearance in a foreign country, pronouncing his message in the hearing of the people. Not just any foreign territory: Nineveh was a byword for brutality and oppression, the seat of the greatest enemy of Israel and Judah. Thus the original readers of the book would surely have shared a ready sympathy for Jonah in this gruelling mission to journey into the territory of evil incarnate.

The great city of Nineveh

Nineveh Ruins

Mosul

The city of Nineveh occupied a central position on the great highway between the Mediterranean and the Indian Ocean, thus uniting the East and the West; its location on the east bank of the River Tigris proved an ideal stopping place for north-south traffic. The city attracted wealth from many parts of the world, so that it became the greatest of all ancient cities, enjoying the status of being the capital of the Assyrian Empire in the last hundred years of its dominance.

Nineveh is now part of Mosul, on the opposite bank of the Tigris, the second largest city in the Republic of Iraq (see above). Mosul was the first city to be captured by so-called Islamic State (Isis). In July 2014 the Sunni jihadists blew up the traditional tomb and shrine of Nebi Yunus, the prophet Jonah, even though Jonah is celebrated in the Qur'an as a righteous preacher of the message of God. Suddenly Nineveh and Jonah were back in the headline news.

Nineveh was destroyed in 612 BC by a coalition of Babylonians, Medes and assorted allies, and then lay abandoned until the middle of the nineteenth century. In 1842, the French Consul General at Mosul, Paul-Émile Botta began his search of the ruins situated on the opposite bank of the Tigris. In 1847 the young British adventurer Austen Henry Layard explored these ruins, unearthing the palace and famous library of King Ashurbanipal with over 200,000 cuneiform clay tablets and stunning rock reliefs.

On many of the rock reliefs are carvings of a traditional duty of all Assyrian kings: to protect the people from wild animals, the fiercest of these being the lion. The finest Assyrian carvings of the lion-hunt are the famous stone reliefs from the North Palace at Nineveh (see pp. 25–27) belonging to Ashurbanipal (668–631 BC) and now in the British Museum. Ashurbanipal decorated the passages of his palace with these lively scenes, mostly illustrating his own achievements of the lion-hunt – one of the earliest examples of the "selfie". As noted by Sarah Collins:

> Yet the main purpose of the reliefs was not decorations but the glorification of king and empire. They show an idealised world in which the king is a fearless hunter and the Assyrians defeat and punish their enemies without loss of life or injury to themselves.[4]

Ashurbanipal is also renowned for the vast library he created at Nineveh. Copies of some of the greatest literary works from ancient Iraq, including the *Epic of Gilgamesh* as well as writings on astrology, medicine and mathematics, are among the collection in the Assyrian Rooms of the British Museum.

---

[4] S. Collins (ed.), *The Wonders of Ancient Mesopotamia* (Melbourne: Museum Victoria, 2012), 33. See also J. Reade, *Assyrian Sculpture* (London: British Museum Press, 2012), 72-9.

Fourteen years after the death of Ashurbanipal, Nineveh suffered a defeat from which it never recovered. Extensive traces of ash, representing the destruction of the city, have been found in many parts of the acropolis. After 612 BC the city ceased to be important, its provinces divided among the victors.

Before its destruction the prophet Nahum prophesied against Nineveh, the fiercest and most despised enemy of both Israel and Judah:

> I will throw filth at you
>
> and treat you with contempt,
>
> and make you a spectacle.
>
> Then all who see you will shrink from you and say,
>
> "Nineveh is devastated; who will bemoan her?"
>
> Where shall I seek comforters for you?
>
> (Nahum 3: 6-7)

Crossing boundaries

Paradoxically, it is Jonah who proves to be Nineveh's comforter. Nowhere else in the Old Testament is there mention of Jonah's call, his mission to Nineveh, or to any other events mentioned in the book of Jonah. Our prophet is commanded to cross boundaries he would never have imagined even approaching, not just geographical but theological: to go and personally hold out the offer of repentance and consolation to the Assyrian people of Nineveh, the power that wiped his own people off the face of the earth. Although the content of Jonah's message is doom-laden, its effect, as Jonah rightly suspects, will be the salvation of the city and its people.

Nations, ancient and modern, are defined by boundaries, and belonging to a defined territory clearly influences people's sense of who they are: geography is an intrinsic part of personal and national identity. A person's identity is clearly linked with homeland, a place attaching them to a sense of belonging, to roots, to land, to family, to language, to culture and sometimes to religion. Identity and homeland, however, particularly when boundaries are threatened by invasion or expanded by conquest, can act as a prompt to war.

In 2 Kings 14 Jonah pronounces the word of God to King Jeroboam II and Israel's ancient borders are restored – a sure sign of God's blessing and assurance for the security of his people now settled within the boundaries of their own land, even if this time is short lived. Our Jonah has to leave the security of his own land and kinsfolk to act as God's messenger in foreign territory. Jonah's God is not only the God of Israel but the Lord of all the nations of the earth who is not confined to any boundary or restricted to any national identity. This God is not the unmoved mover, but a God who notices and is moved to action: thus he sends his Hebrew prophet to cry out against the pagan people of the city and confront them with their wrongdoing.

For Jonah to follow this summons and cross this frontier is a grim and demanding task.

Identity, direction, outlook

But Jonah set out to flee to Tarshish from the presence of the LORD.

(Jonah 1:3a)

Commanded by God to go north-east by land to Nineveh, five hundred and fifty miles away, Jonah decides to go due west by sea to Tarshish, 2,500 miles away. Desperate to escape from the presence of God, Jonah is also fleeing from his own identity and mission. We all know that this can happen in life: we can all suffer a sudden loss of enthusiasm for the mission, not least when it leads us to the wrong address and the wrong community. Whatever obedience Jonah showed to the word of God before this time, he now feels he can no longer comply.

Jonah is challenged in three different ways. Firstly, in his identity: as a prophet he is running away not only from the word of God but from his true self. Secondly, in his direction: his destination is specified by God, but he elects to take the opposite course. Thirdly, in his outlook: a prophet's outlook is supposed to be formed and dominated by the word of God, whereas Jonah's outlook is now formed and dominated by his own theological thinking and his fear.

Jonah, of course, is not only a prophet – his identity is made up of other affiliations such as loyalty to country, race, religion, family, friends, home province, and a litany of other attachments. None of these allegiances is equally strong. In his study of the nature of identity Amin Maalouf comments:

> Every individual is a meeting ground for many different allegiances, and sometimes these loyalties conflict with one another and confront the person who harbours them with difficult choices…

> While there is always a certain hierarchy among the elements that go to make up individual identities, that hierarchy is not immutable; it changes with time, and in so doing, brings about fundamental changes in behaviour.[5]

Certainly the hierarchy of Jonah's identities shifts as his governing identity as a prophet is displaced from its pre-eminence, even though what he does in fleeing God is still related to that identity. His identity as a theologian now surpasses that of his identity as a prophet: how he believes God should act becomes more important to him than what God has commanded him to do.

While Jonah knows that Israel has benefited in the past from the Lord who repents, Jonah objects to this repentance being extended indiscriminately to other people, especially the wicked people of Nineveh. Jonah believes that God is too lavish with the gift of his mercy. He acts on this belief as he abandons his prophetic mission.

---

[5] Amin Maalouf, *On Identity* (London: Harvill Press, 2000), 5, 12.

I don't think Jonah abandons his identity as a prophet. Reflecting generally on identity and selfhood Peter Wagner comments:

> In each individual life there is a minimum of continuity, most basically of bodily existence, and there are always discontinuities. To pose the question of identity means to consider whether particular changes can be seen within a framework of continuity or as a rupture. A conversion, for instance, may mean for one person a conclusive reinterpretation of her or his own religiosity and spirituality, for someone else, however, a break with the entire preceding life and identity.[6]

While Jonah tries to make a break with his preceding life and identity, it is certainly not a final rupture since he will be recalled to his mission later in the narrative. Jonah has not lost his faith in God; he is not creating a different self, nor has he become someone else; he is in flight from the direction God has commanded him to take as his prophet.

---

[6] Peter Wagner, "Identity and Selfhood as a Problématique" in *Identities: Time, Difference and Boundaries*, ed. Heidrun Friese (Oxford: Berghahn Books, 2000), 48.

Conflict is established in this opening paragraph of the book, so we the readers are invited into the drama of flight and the psychological conflict within Jonah, knowing that this struggle is not peculiar to Jonah but touches everyone. We could see Jonah's conflict outlined in this way:

What Jonah is called to do		What Jonah does
to be a prophet of the Lord	identity	becomes a runaway prophet
to go east to Nineveh	direction	he heads west to Tarshish
dominated by the word of God	outlook	dominated by his own belief and fear

Jonah is in meltdown:

→ About who he is

→ About where he is going

→ About what determines his choices.

Each of us has to face the three questions:

→ Who am I?

→ Where am I going in life?

→ What forms my outlook on life?

Jonah's conflict admirably illustrates the fundamental challenge that we all face in our lives. The lived answers to these three questions determine the authenticity of our lives. And the challenge always is to ensure that these three defining characteristics are on speaking terms with one another and that there is no disconnection or contradiction between them.

The challenge is that the choices we make and the roads we take are consistent with who we claim to be as our governing identity; that the way we look at the world and other people is consistent with who we are and our chosen course of life. Naturally, for all of us, this consistency can gradually fracture over time or break down completely.

As the book of Jonah teaches, when these three markers – identity, direction and outlook – are consistent with each other and in working order, this is what is seen as integrity of life; when there is coherence between who we are and the choices we make; when there is compatibility between who we are and the roads we take in life. This is Jonah's challenge: to be authentic. In his classic study of alienation and the psychological dislocation of a number of modern characters, Colin Wilson could have been summarising the challenge for Jonah:

> The Outsider is not sure who he is. He has found an "I", but it is not his true "I". His main business is to find his way back to himself.[7]

---

[7] Colin Wilson, *The Outsider* (London: Phoenix, 1967), 147.

Jonah goes down

He went down to Joppa and found a ship going to Tarshish; so he paid his fare and went on board, to go with them to Tarshish, away from the presence of the LORD.

(Jonah 1:3b)

Jonah goes down to Joppa; he will go down to the hold of the ship; he will go down to the depth of the sea: from this point onwards Jonah is going down. In trying to flee from the presence of God, the words of the psalmist are lost on him:

> O where can I go from your spirit,
>   or where can I flee from your face?
> If I climb the heavens, you are there.
>   If I lie in the grave, you are there.
>
> If I take the wings of the dawn
>   and dwell at the sea's furthest end,
> even there your hand would lead me,
>   your right hand would hold me fast.
>
> (Psalm 139:7-10; Grail translation)

Jonah's goal is to escape from God's presence. Distance from God is Jonah's driving goal. As Rosemary Nixon comments: "Adam *hid himself* from God's presence; Cain *went out* from God's presence, and Jonah *fled*. These are images of human beings afraid of their calling."[8] Thus Jonah heads for the ancient harbour of Joppa (now Jaffa, south of Tel Aviv), the only natural harbour at the time on the eastern coast between Phoenicia to the north and Egypt to the south. Being a large harbour city, Joppa was probably inhabited mostly by Gentiles since Israel was never a seagoing nation. It might be worth noting that it was in this city that Simon bar-Jonah, Peter, received the revelation that no one was profane or unclean (Acts 10:9-16. 28) and that God's grace was for every human being.

---

[8] Rosemary Nixon, *The Message of Jonah* (Nottingham: Inter-Varsity Press, 2009), 69.

Jonah buys a ticket, choosing a boat going to Tarshish – a name mentioned three times as his destination. King Solomon took great pride in his ships which were manned by foreigners: "Once every three years the fleet of ships of Tarshish used to come bringing gold, silver, ivory, apes, and peacocks" (1 Kings 10:25). Jonah does not seek out a boat heading up the regional coast of Israel: Tarshish was 2,500 miles distant, on the other side of the Great Sea, the Mediterranean, on the south-west coast of Spain – the point being that it was seriously far away.

Jonah leaves his family, his country and, he hopes, his God. If God is only the God of Israel, in leaving Israel he might manage to leave God behind him. There was a popular belief among many nations that a country's god was limited to that territory: thus when people were impressed by another country's god, they would often take that country's soil with them in the hope that the god of that land would travel with them. We can see this following Naaman's healing: when the commander Naaman travels to Israel and his leprosy is healed by the prophet Elisha, Naaman asks the prophet to have two mule-loads of earth to take back with him to his own country, "for your servant will no longer offer burnt offering or sacrifice to any god except the LORD" (2 Kings 5:17).

Whatever is in Jonah's baggage when he flees, we can be certain that there is one thing missing: soil from Israel.

Why does Jonah flee?

So why does Jonah flee? One could argue that given the content of his message, Jonah should be delighted to announce the final doom of the Assyrian Empire. The readers are not told the reason for Jonah's flight until later in 4:2, perhaps deliberately to build up sympathy for our reluctant prophet risking his life in the Assyrian den of iniquity. The writer postpones telling of an earlier argument when Jonah received his commission:

> Is not this what I said while I was still in my own country? That is why I fled to Tarshish at the beginning; for I knew that you are a gracious God and merciful, slow to anger, and abounding in steadfast love, and ready to relent from punishing.
>
> (Jonah 4:2)

Jonah flees to deprive God offering mercy to the city of Nineveh. Paradoxically, Jonah is a good theologian: he anticipates the fullness of the Gospel. Pope Francis put it axiomatically when he wrote of how the Church must reflect the universal mercy of God: "The Church must be a place of mercy freely given, where everyone can feel welcomed, loved, forgiven and encouraged to live the good life of the Gospel" (*Evangelii Gaudium*, 114).

Like Pope Francis, Jonah believes in the stubborn mercy of God and in his steadfast love. These, Jonah believes, are the governing attributes of God, qualities which will lead God to change his mind about the punishment. Strangely, this belief leads Jonah to be fearful: were he to go to Nineveh to pronounce God's affliction and the people repented, then, he is certain, God would relent. Jonah is not inclined to play his part in the drama, insisting on God's certain punishment only then to see God turning up as the maestro of mercy, heaping forgiveness on everyone and everything in sight.

This, of course, would leave Jonah looking like a fool and some people might question if he was a genuine prophet. In God's instruction to Moses, the characteristic of a true prophet is described:

> You may say to yourself, "How can we recognize a word that the LORD has not spoken?" If a prophet speaks in the name of the LORD but the thing does not take place or prove true, it is a word that the LORD has not spoken.
> (Deuteronomy 18:21-22)

If what Jonah predicted did not happen, would that make him a false prophet? Jonah does not want to appear either false or foolish; he does not want to lose face; he wants to avoid being proved spectacularly wrong. As a prophet Jonah believes that what he proclaims with authority must surely happen, especially to the sworn enemy of his people. Jonah is a modern: he wants to look good, keep his celebrity status intact and be respected for his unerring insights. He has an overriding compulsion to be right. Playing the fool is not part of his self-understanding; neither is it part of how he understands his vocation.

From Major to Minor

And perhaps that is why he is a minor prophet, ever fretful of his self-image. Look at the Major Prophets and their utter indifference to how others regard them.

Think of the prophet **Isaiah**.

At that time the LORD had spoken to Isaiah son of Amoz, saying, "Go, and loose the sackcloth from your loins and take your sandals off your feet", and he had done so, walking naked and barefoot. Then the LORD said, "Just as my servant Isaiah has walked naked and barefoot for three years as a sign and a portent against Egypt and Ethiopia, so shall the king of Assyria lead away the Egyptians as captives and the Ethiopians as exiles, both the young and the old, naked and barefoot, with buttocks uncovered, to the shame of Egypt.

(Isaiah 20:2-4)

The great prophet Isaiah is commanded to walk around naked for three years, an embarrassing street theatre show, acting out before the people the fate that surely awaits them at the hands of the King of Assyria. Today you would be arrested for indecent exposure. Three years, wandering around naked: who would ask the prophet to be the keynote speaker at their upcoming conference? Clearly Isaiah is beyond worrying about his reputation; he acts out in his body the coming nightmare of the people.

Think of the prophet **Jeremiah.**

This word came to Jeremiah from the LORD. Thus the LORD said to me: Make yourself a yoke of straps and bars, and put them on your neck… Now I have given all these lands into the hand of King Nebuchadnezzar of Babylon, my servant, and I have given him even the wild animals of the field to serve him. All the nations shall serve him and his son and his grandson, until the time of his own land comes; then many nations and great kings shall make him their slave.

(Jeremiah 27:1-2. 6-7)

Like Isaiah, the prophet Jeremiah is commanded to become street theatre. He stumbles like a beast of burden around the city streets, wearing a wooden yoke with straps and bars. If you met Jeremiah outside the supermarket, would you give him the name of a good psychiatrist? And when the false prophets take off his wooden yoke and break it, the yoke now becomes one of iron. He is symbolising a warning to the people that they will bend their necks and be overpowered by the yoke of Babylon.

Think of the prophet **Ezekiel**.

The word of the LORD came to me... prepare for yourself an exile's baggage, and go into exile by day in their sight; you shall go like an exile from your place to another place in their sight. Perhaps they will understand, though they are a rebellious house. You shall bring out your baggage by day in their sight, as baggage for exile; and you shall go out yourself at evening in their sight, as those do who go into exile. Dig through the wall in their sight, and carry the baggage through it. In their sight you shall lift the baggage on your shoulder, and carry it out in the dark; you shall cover your face, so that you may not see the land; for I have made you a sign for the house of Israel. I did just as I was commanded.

(Ezekiel 12:1. 3-7)

Ezekiel is commanded by God to pack a bundle of belongings during the day and leave like a fugitive at night. He has to make sure that the people are looking. He is commanded to make a hole in the wall and go through it. Imagine you are there: you might be tempted to say, "Ezekiel, there is a good door there. Hinges are fine. Why are you making a hole in the wall?" Ezekiel is performing the mime of the emigrant, acting out the coming time when the people will become exiles, each with a little knapsack on their backs, being led out through the broken walls of their ruined city.

These Major Prophets use mime and street theatre and drama to act out the scenes they have been commanded by the Lord, to warn the people of the tragedy that awaits them. The prophets need dazzling gesture to ensure that they can command the attention of the people. To everyone else they may look nervous wrecks or just plain mad. But they are not worried about their personal image or how they appear to others: they are totally taken up in communicating the truth they have been commanded to act out.

By comparison, our sensitive Jonah is not in their league. His energy is devoted to protecting his persona and guarding his image – hence his flight from the presence of God and from his difficult mission. Unlike Ezekiel he cannot say: "I did just what I was commanded." Jonah does indeed arise and go, but heads for a destination he believes will give him shelter and provide a hiding-place from God. Jonah is heading for a wet surprise.

All at sea

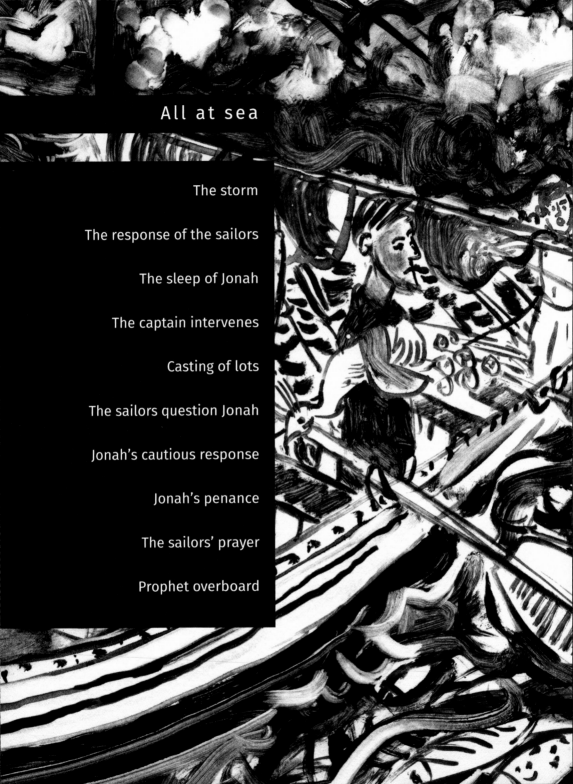

All at sea

The storm

The response of the sailors

The sleep of Jonah

The captain intervenes

Casting of lots

The sailors question Jonah

Jonah's cautious response

Jonah's penance

The sailors' prayer

Prophet overboard

The storm

But the LORD hurled a great wind upon the sea, and such a mighty storm came upon the sea that the ship threatened to break up.

(Jonah 1:4)

In the opening sentence of the book of Jonah we hear God speak; now we see God act, dramatically intervening as he unleashes the power of disorder by hurling a great wind at the sea. If Jonah is the fugitive, God is the hunter in spectacular pursuit of the prophet who thinks he can escape the divine reach. As Jonah sets his personal compass for distance from God, that same God turns towards Jonah, refusing to abandon his prophet. God does not allow Jonah's rebellion to have the last word. The chase is on, not to condemn Jonah for his desertion but to summon him back to his original calling - an image of hope for all who travel a similar route.

Jonah's struggle with his vocation is one which speaks to legions of people as they strive to juggle their vocation with their personal preferences. The distinguished writer and Trappist monk Thomas Merton reflected that to make sense of his own vocation and struggle, he looked to the story of Jonah for remedy. The paradox of Jonah's life became the paradox of Merton's reluctant response to his calling as a monk. As Jonah went in the opposite direction of his calling from God, Merton felt sympathy with the fugitive prophet:

> I found myself with an almost uncontrollable desire to go in the opposite direction. God pointed one way and all my "ideals" pointed in the other.[9]

The ancient story of Jonah threw light on Merton's personal dilemma, reminding me of the wonderful lines spoken by Hector in Alan Bennett's *The History Boys*:

> The best moments in reading are when you come across something - a thought, a feeling, a way of looking at things - that you'd thought special, particular to you. And here it is, set down by someone else, a person you've never met, maybe even someone long dead. And it's as if a hand has come out and taken yours.[10]

---

[9] Thomas Merton, *The Sign of Jonas* (New York: Harcourt Brace, 1953), 11.

[10] *The History Boys*, Nicholas Hytner, dir. (20th Century Fox, 2006).

Jonah's hand found Merton's hand. For Merton, as with Jonah, the struggle between the competing voices of vocation and preference will lead to a discovery. Merton's life was interrupted by a voice he did not summon but he eventually embraced the voice, accepting it as a true calling which he followed to the end of his life.

As Jonah's vacation to Spain is cancelled by a storm, so his vocation as a prophet will be saved.

The tempest is so fierce that the ship, as if it were a thinking person calculating this unexpected menace, threatens to break up. The writer's personification of the ship may be a deliberate device in making the ship one of God's accomplices in sabotaging Jonah's escape - as later in 1:15 the writer speaks of the personification of the sea in similar terms, "the sea ceased from its raging." Jonah attempted to make good his escape through ship and sea and wind: now all three conspire with God to end Jonah's flight.

The response of the sailors

Then the sailors were afraid, and each cried to his god. They threw the cargo that was in the ship into the sea, to lighten it for them.

(Jonah 1:5a)

As the raging sea tosses the ship about, fear grips the sailors as each one cries out to his god for help: no doubt there were as many nations and religions represented on the ship as there were sailors. The sailors make their desperate pleas to their gods because, although they have endured wind and storms before, they sense the supernatural character of this tempest which threatens the lives of all on board. This is no ordinary onslaught by the elements: there must be a hidden meaning in this great storm. The sailors' terror, confusion and hope are all reflected in these verses of Psalm 107:23-29:

> Some went down to the sea in ships,
>   doing business on the mighty waters;
> they saw the deeds of the LORD,
>   his wondrous works in the deep.
> For he commanded and raised the stormy wind,
>   which lifted up the waves of the sea.
> They mounted up to heaven, they went down to the depths;
>   their courage melted away in their calamity;
> they reeled and staggered like drunkards,
>   and were at their wits' end.
> Then they cried to the LORD in their trouble,
>   and he brought them out from their distress;
> he made the storm be still,
>   and the waves of the sea were hushed.

Having appealed to a range of deities, the sailors know the sea has not been stilled and the waves have not been hushed. With their world about to be shattered, the sailors now get to work, lightening the ship's load by jettisoning anything not essential. In the ancient world, apart from imperial galleys and fighting ships, all long-haul ships were cargo vessels with their vast, rounded hulls, to spread the weight of their consignment. There were no dedicated passenger ships: travellers, like Jonah, would have to join a cargo ship heading in their direction.

The journey to Tarshish would have taken about a year and on arrival the sailors would have delivered their goods and loaded a new cargo for the return journey. The livelihood of the sailors depends on delivering the merchandise on board: as God hurled the wind at the sea, in the face of this life-threatening tempest the sailors now hurl the cargo overboard – and a year's livelihood – as they try to save the ship and the lives of all on board. Their values are forcibly clarified in favour of human life and survival.

The sleep of Jonah

Jonah, meanwhile, had gone down into the hold of the ship and had lain down, and was fast asleep.

(Jonah 1:5b)

The scene now shifts below deck, to focus on the reason for this disaster and the one person who is visiting ruin on all around him. In the midst of the ship being battered by wind and sea, together with the sailors' frantic activity, we are now told that not all hands are on deck – Jonah is fast asleep in the ship's hold. He dwells inside his own bubble. Both self-awareness and recognition of the chaos he has caused are lost on him; he inhabits only the miniature geography of his own story. Commenting on the text, Phyllis Trible highlights the comparison between the activity of the sailors and the inactivity of Jonah:

> On the deck the sailors move from inner emotion to outward cry to vigorous action; below the deck Jonah moves from action to inaction to total withdrawal. As they increase, he decreases… the asymmetry sharpens the antithesis between the sailors and Jonah.[11]

---

[11] Phyllis Trible, *Rhetorical Criticism: Context, Method, and the Book of Jonah* (Minneapolis: Fortress, 1994), 135.

While the pagan sailors sought deliverance in prayer, the prophet of God seeks oblivion in sleep. Jonah's zoning out, which effectively cuts out everyone and everything around him, seems strange in the midst of such turmoil. With due respect to St Jerome in his *Commentary on Jonah*, it seems unlikely that "Jonah is so peaceful, so calm, his spirit is so at rest that he goes down to the heart of the ship to enjoy a peaceful sleep."[12] So what is this deep sleep?

I would posit the sleep of Jonah is not peaceful rest but anguished withdrawal – the compulsion to remove himself from the gloom and the growing threat of his surrounding world. The Greeks had a special name for this condition: *scotosis*, which refers to elected blindness and the hardening of the heart against unwelcome insight. *Scotosis* is the struggle to ward off knowledge that will surely upset our chosen way of viewing the world. In that sense, it is a response to deep anxiety: because we realise that we are not yet what we are called to be, we are either in the painful process of transcending our fragmented selves or on the road to self-destruction. Clearly Jonah is on the road to self-destruction.

---

[12] St Jerome, *Commentary on Jonah*, Ancient Bible Commentaries in English, ed. John Litteral and translated by Robin MacGregor (Kentucky: Litteral's Christian Library Publications, 2014), 13.

Commenting on the repeated image of Jonah "going down", the philosopher and psychoanalyst Eric Fromm shared his insight:

> We find a sequence of symbols which follow one another: going down into the ship, going down into the ship's belly, going down to sleep, going down to the ocean, and going down to the fish's belly. All these symbols stand for the same inner experience: for a condition of being protected and isolated, of safe withdrawal from communication with other human beings.[13]

Clearly the deep sleep of Jonah makes sense – to Jonah. The son of Amittai is being challenged in three ways:

→   His **identity** (who is he?)

→   His **direction** (where is he going?)

→   His **outlook** (what shapes the way he looks at the world?)

In choosing sleep he is electing to shut out the three challenges that go to the heart of the person God has commanded him to be, where God has commanded him to go and the message God has commanded him to proclaim:

→   His identity as a prophet of God

→   His direction, to go to the great city of Nineveh

→   His outlook, to preach the word of the Lord.

---

[13] E. Fromm, *The Forgotten Language* (New York: Grove Press, 1957), 22.

The captain intervenes

The captain came and said to him, "What are you doing sound asleep? Get up, call on your god! Perhaps he will spare us a thought so that we do not perish."

(Jonah 1:6)

If the cargo is kept mostly in the hold of the ship, where Jonah is sleeping below deck, it seems not unlikely that Jonah is discovered by the sailors in the process of clearing out the cargo as they empty the ship's hold. At any rate, Jonah is interrupted by the captain of the ship, a new character in the drama: his is the first human word we hear in the story.

The captain demands an explanation to why Jonah is asleep - an explanation he does not receive. Since Jonah shares the same danger as everyone else, why does he not pray? The pagan captain commands the religious figure to pray to his god: "Get up, call on your god! Perhaps he will spare us a thought so that we do not perish." Since all else has failed, all other prayers unheeded, the captain hopes that Jonah's unknown god might deliver all of them from peril. He does not yet know that Jonah is the source of their problem; he desperately hopes that if Jonah moves from total inattention – from sleep and silence into prayer – this last attempt might prove their salvation.

If Jonah responds, the narrative does not tell us. The runaway prophet is doing his best to escape from God, so he is hardly inclined now to reopen communication with his mission controller. In being found and challenged by the captain, Jonah wants to remain lost to God and be left in peace. Those who want to remain unchallenged in their mission rarely pray to God.

Often part of the burden of suffering is that people don't talk to one another. Even though they might be together, facing the same threat, they can remain isolated and mute, sharing their pain with no one.

As Shakespeare advises in *Macbeth*:

> Merciful heaven!
> What, man! Ne'er pull your hat upon your brows;
> Give sorrow words; the grief that does not speak
> Whispers the o'erfraught heart and bids it break.[14]

The prophet does not give sorrow words; his grief does not speak but is covered in sleep as he chooses not to pay attention. Jonah elects sleep to avoid attending the tragedy that is befalling him, the ship and all on board.

Were Jonah to pray, calling upon the name of the Lord and asking for his help, the fugitive prophet would be reminding himself not only about who God is but of the kind of person he should be. Prayer not only reveals God to us but reveals us to ourselves. And since Jonah is in flight not only from God but from his true self, he craves a reintroduction to neither.

---

[14] William Shakespeare, *Macbeth*, Act IV, scene iii.

Casting of lots

The sailors said to one another, "Come, let us cast lots, so that we may know on whose account this calamity has come upon us." So they cast lots, and the lot fell on Jonah.

(Jonah 1:7)

Having appealed to their gods with no discernible result, the sailors now confer with each other, agreeing that the fairest way forward for all is to cast lots to identify the person who has brought this disaster on all of them. The casting of lots was the only form of divination allowed in Israel in order to uncover the divine will: "The lot is cast into the lap, but the decision is the LORD's alone" (Proverbs 16:33). It was also a popular way of discernment throughout the ancient Near East.

One way of conducting this process was to collect small stones, mark each to identify every person in the target group, and then place the stones in some kind of container like a large sieve. Not unlike the lottery (here in the UK), the receptacle was then shaken until one stone fell out, identifying an individual.[15] Having done everything they could, the sailors now use this agreed ritual: the result, beyond their control, is under divine direction and it will surely identify not only the culprit but the god who threatens them all.

Jonah remains strangely and stubbornly silent throughout this ritual, happening in the midst of a vicious storm. He hopes to remain faceless, anonymous, hidden. He could have easily stepped forward and intervened, shown solidarity with his fellow travellers and confessed to them that he was responsible for the whole chaotic scene and their endangerment. Although up to now his risks have hardly been calculated, perhaps our reckless prophet is taking a calculated risk that the result will not be divinely driven but be random, singling out some useful victim, leaving Jonah securely in camouflage.

The ritual of casting lots commences:

The storm still rages; the divination proceeds; the stones are marked; they are collected and placed together; the container is shaken; everyone waits; the first stone drops; Jonah is singled out by lot.

The silence that Jonah thought might protect him is now broken; without saying a word, Jonah is exposed and his name is announced as the person responsible for imperilling the lives of everyone on board. Jonah is not one victim among a boatload of victims: he is the single cause of the chaos everyone is enduring. Now identified, he can no longer hide from himself, from the captain, from the crew or from God.

---

[15] Anne Marie Kitz, "The Hebrew Terminology of Lot Casting and Its Ancient Near Eastern Context" in *Catholic Biblical Quarterly* 62 (2000), 214.

The sailors question Jonah

Then they said to him, "Tell us why this calamity has come upon us. What is your occupation? Where do you come from? What is your country? And of what people are you?"

(Jonah 1:8)

Given the life-threatening circumstances they are braving, these pagan sailors emerge as extraordinarily honourable men. Their instinct is not to punish Jonah by dismissing him overboard as cargo: they suspect that there is a destructive power associated with their passenger, so they proceed warily. The sailors now know who is responsible and they cry out not for vengeance but for understanding, "Tell us why this calamity has come upon us." They do not confront Jonah with the obvious question: "What have you done?" The least they deserve is an answer to the question: "Why are we the victims of a tragedy we have not brought upon ourselves?"

The barrage of questions continues, asking about Jonah's occupation, his hometown, his country, and his race – all of which might reveal the hidden identity of the passenger and the god who has been offended. In the midst of a storm and afraid for their lives, the sailors' list of questions, however pressing, seems overly polite and expansive when they want answers to only two: "Who is your God? How have you offended him?"

Jonah's cautious response

"I am a Hebrew," he replied. "I worship the LORD, the God of heaven, who made the sea and the dry land." Then the men were even more afraid, and said to him, "What is this that you have done!" For the men knew that he was fleeing from the presence of the LORD, because he had told them so.

(Jonah 1:9-10)

Jonah speaks for the first time in the narrative and is, unsurprisingly, oblique in his answers. What he avoids telling them are two key characteristics about himself: his identity as a prophet of God and the direction he has been commanded to take, to bring God's word to Nineveh. Nor does he tell them where he is from. The cautious prophet tells them that he is a Hebrew – not a stunning revelation, I think, in the circumstances – referring to the usual name foreigners used when talking of Israelites and, conversely, the name Israelites normally used when identifying themselves to foreigners.

Jonah moves away from revealing more about himself and now talks about his God – not a local deity confined to a particular space or a distinct cause, but the one who is not only God of heaven but the creator of everything under the firmament – the sea and the land. Jonah's God is omnipotent over the whole cosmos; nothing is beyond his rule or reach. In confessing his allegiance to the creator of the sea, the sailors understand this to mean that Jonah's God must be the creator of the storm that threatens all of them. This revelation makes them greatly afraid.

It is difficult to know what Jonah means by "I worship the Lord" when he is in total flight from the same Lord. Jonah's acknowledged veneration of this God of the cosmos leads the sailors to express their moral outrage and exclaim in disbelief: "What is this that you have done!" The pagan sailors seem to have more moral sense than the religious prophet and they are appalled at Jonah's self-serving behaviour. They cannot imagine treating their local gods in such a dismissive way. Why would Jonah, who worships this cosmic deity, defy him and endanger the lives of blameless people? In fleeing from a sovereign Lord, using the captain and crew of this ship, did Jonah not pause to think about the consequences of his action? Their key question follows Jonah's reported admission that he is fleeing from the presence of God.

The pagan sailors are clearer than Jonah about the magnitude of his flight from God, not least because the prophet's bolt for freedom has affected all of them in the most menacing way. Jonah's decision was not a cloistered one, free of social consequences; rather, his decision has not only caused decent people great distress but has also endangered their lives. Jonah still regards himself as an innocent. I am reminded of a sentence from Graham Greene's *The Quiet American*:

> Innocence always calls mutely for protection when we would
>
> be so much wiser to guard ourselves against it: innocence is
>
> like a dumb leper who has lost his bell, wandering the world,
>
> meaning no harm.[16]

The innocent Jonah wanders the world meaning no harm, but causing chaos. Good people can cause chaos – you only have to live in a community a few hours to discover that. Jonah learns this not through self-reflection but through confrontation: sometimes people have to be challenged, as St Paul was, with the destructive consequences of their behaviour before they come to self-awareness and a change of heart. With the protestations of the sailors, Jonah is roused to the recognition that he is no innocent, but is responsible for the whole tragedy, jeopardising the lives of all on board.

---

[16] Graham Greene, *The Quiet American* (London: Reprint Society, 1957), 34.

Jonah's penance

Then they said to him, "What shall we do to you, that the sea may quiet down for us?" For the sea was growing more and more tempestuous. He said to them, "Pick me up and throw me into the sea; then the sea will quiet down for you; for I know it is because of me that this great storm has come upon you." Nevertheless the men rowed hard to bring the ship back to land, but they could not, for the sea grew more and more stormy against them.

(Jonah 1:11-13)

The sailors dream of quitting this terrible tempest and returning to peace and quiet on dry land. Given that they now know Jonah to be the cause of the disaster, the sailors question Jonah further, though they remain staggeringly polite as they invite their passenger to offer ideas about what to do with him. While they know that everything they have tried has not worked, they do not know how to appease the prophet's God. That said, they are committed to taking responsibility: given Jonah's inaction and the gathering torment of the sea, the sailors believe that *they* have to do something.

The sailors' real fear and protests prompt Jonah to be honest about his personal responsibility for the calamity that engulfs them all – that, at least, is a development. While the sailors appreciate that the tempest may not quieten down for Jonah, they realistically ask "that the sea may quiet down for us?"

Jonah makes his confession, admitting that he is the cause of the chaos. Reality is now beginning to impress itself on him; his game of hide-and-seek is over; his identity is re-emerging. Then Jonah provides the penance, although what is needed is not penance but repentance: penance without repentance is simply self-punishment. Rather than casting himself into the hands of a merciful Lord, Jonah specifies the penance – that the sailors throw him into the rough seas. He takes their earlier point, adding "then the sea will quiet down for you".

The penance, of course, must be carried out by the sailors: Jonah cannot manage his own penance, asking them to take responsibility in sacrificing his life. He remains passive; the decision must be theirs. In not seeing any way forward, Jonah opts for assisted suicide as an exit from his personal crisis. Why does he not acknowledge his wrongdoing to God and repent, so that the seas would be calm again and the sailors could return him to Joppa? Why does he still stubbornly refuse to talk to the God he says he worships? What is his aversion to seeing what everyone else sees? Why is he still unwilling to follow his vocation and mission, preferring death? Why does he not follow his own suggestion and jump overboard himself? Why does he give the penance for his sin to the sailors, involving them in a communal act of murder? Why does he not do something himself? Jonah reminds me of one of Tolstoy's characters who says:

> Why have I come here? Where am I taking myself? Why and where am I escaping? I'm running away from something dreadful and cannot escape it. I am always with myself, and it's I who am my own tormentor. Here I am, the whole of me … It is myself I am weary of and find intolerable, and such a torment. I want to fall asleep and forget myself and cannot. I cannot get away from myself![17]

Jonah has no hope that he will be delivered from the tempest – that will not happen until he grows into his true identity as a prophet, until he follows the direction God has given him, until the word of God, not his own fear, shapes his outlook. In avoiding this he has catapulted others into a conflict not of their own making; in avoiding his true vocation he has imperilled the lives of others.

Rather than die to his own theological outlook, Jonah seeks his own death by drowning; he wants to be treated as the excess baggage that has already been thrown overboard. Keeping his pride intact, he prefers annihilation to repentance. Surprisingly, he does not pray, acknowledging his foolishness and begging his gracious God for mercy; instead he opts for certain death. And this will not be the last time he opts for death over repentance.

---

[17] L. Tolstoy, "Memoirs of a Madman" in *Tolstoy's Short Fiction*, ed. M. R. Katz (London: W.W. Norton, 2008), 307.

The sailors are undoubtedly impressive characters, their moderation exemplary: it is not in their job description to throw fee-paying passengers overboard, so they ignore their passenger's proposal and try to row back to land, hoping they can land *everyone* in safety. The harder they row, the rougher the storm becomes: "for the sea grew more and more stormy against them." The sea conspires with God against their brave struggle. The sailors' kindness is misplaced, their tolerance misguided; their effort useless. Why? They

are trying to solve Jonah's problem for him while Jonah does nothing, remaining an observer of their struggle on his behalf. Of course he never thanks them for their graciousness and hard effort, remaining imprisoned within the boundaries of his own little world.

The sailors' prayer

Then they cried out to the LORD, "Please, O LORD, we pray, do not let us perish on account of this man's life. Do not make us guilty of innocent blood; for you, O LORD, have done as it pleased you."

(Jonah 1:14)

The sailors concede defeat. Resigned to follow Jonah's suggestion, they first pray to Jonah's God, seeking absolution before their act, while the prophet maintains an awkward silence. The first prayer to the Lord in this story comes from the Gentile sailors. Whereas Jonah's fear led him to flee from God, the sailors' fear leads them to attend God: paradoxically, they have become Jonah's converts. Although Jonah ran away to avoid converting the pagans of Nineveh, he has now converted the pagan sailors - not because of his moral strength but because of his fear and weakness. As he was turning away from God, he turned the pagan sailors towards the same God.

Sometimes it is vulnerability which moves people and stirs them to change; sometimes success and power and strength alienate people and leave them cold as marble because they feel removed from that world of perfection, bogged down as they are in the tear and trudge of life. In a strange way, for the sailors, Jonah's failure makes his faith in the Lord plausible.

Robert Alter comments on how often our struggles take place

> at the intersection of incompatibles – the relative and the absolute, human imperfection and divine perfection, the brawling chaos of historical experience and God's promise to fulfil a design in history. The biblical outlook is informed, I think, by a sense of stubborn contradiction, of a profound and ineradicable untidiness in the nature of things.[18]

Certainly Jonah's solution is untidy, involving as it does the sailors who fear there will be consequences to their decision of throwing Jonah overboard: they don't want to be held responsible for the murder of their passenger. After expressing their trepidation, they express their belief in the sovereignty of God who has controlled everything up to this point. Turning away from their local gods, they are now praying to the God of the heavens and the land and the sea, hoping that in doing what they have to do, they will be his agents. Unlike Jonah, they seek to do the will of the Lord. The God of Jonah, they believe, is behind everything and has done as he pleased. As it states in Psalm 135:6:

> Whatever the Lord pleases, he does,
>
> in heaven and on earth,
>
> in the seas and all deeps.

---

[18] Robert Alter, *The Art of Biblical Narrative* (New York: Basic Books, 1981), 125-126.

Prophet overboard

So they picked Jonah up and threw him into the sea; and the sea ceased from its raging. Then the men feared the LORD even more, and they offered a sacrifice to the LORD and made vows.

(Jonah 1:15-16)

Although reluctant, the sailors follow Jonah's instructions and throw him overboard; when they do, all is suddenly calm. This happens sometimes in a community: one person leaves, tranquillity returns. Sometimes an absence is the most precious gift to the community left behind. Jonah does not jump overboard, taking full responsibility for his action: the sailors discharge his sentence. The sea responds immediately to the sailors' actions, affirming what they have done and answering their earlier wish "that the sea may quiet down for us?"

Their sense of helplessness now evaporates but their fear deepens in the sense that their awe at God's saving activity now dominates their lives. With the restored calm, the Gentile sailors' new faith in God has been rewarded. The awe of these new converts moves to devotion as they offer sacrifice to the Lord and make vows.

71

As Jonah disappears into the depth of the sea, the sailors now disappear from the story. The positive portrayal of the Gentile sailors anticipates the favourable depiction of the king and people of Nineveh: both groups move to acknowledge the power and mercy of the one true Lord, who is not only the God of Israel. As this Lord's power makes people fear, his mercy leads them to a change of heart and mind. Jonah refused to go and save the Gentile people of Nineveh, yet these Gentile sailors did all they could to save Jonah. The good news will be revealed that the mercy of the Lord will not abandon his chosen prophet, but will hunt him and save him even in the depth of the sea.

One is reminded of the opening lines of Francis Thompson's *Hound of Heaven*:

> I fled Him, down the nights and down the days;
>
> > I fled Him, down the arches of the years;
>
> I fled Him, down the labyrinthine ways
>
> > Of my own mind; and in the mist of tears
>
> I hid from Him, and under running laughter.
>
> > Up vistaed hopes I sped;
>
> > And shot, precipitated,
>
> Adown Titanic glooms of chasmèd fears,
>
> From those strong Feet that followed, followed after.
>
> > But with unhurrying chase,
>
> > And unperturbèd pace,
>
> Deliberate speed, majestic instancy,
>
> > They beat—and a Voice beat
>
> > More instant than the Feet—
>
> All things betray thee, who betrayest Me.[19]

---

[19] F. Thompson, *The Hound of Heaven*, (London: George Harrap, 1923), 11-12.

In the deep

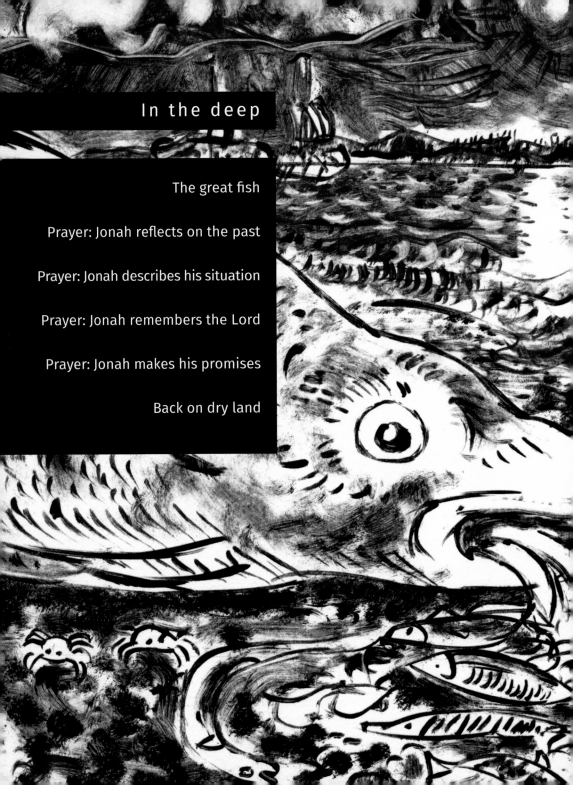

In the deep

The great fish

Prayer: Jonah reflects on the past

Prayer: Jonah describes his situation

Prayer: Jonah remembers the Lord

Prayer: Jonah makes his promises

Back on dry land

The great fish

But the LORD provided a large fish to swallow up Jonah; and Jonah was in the belly of the fish three days and three nights.

(Jonah 1:17)

With the ship, the captain and the crew now retired from the narrative, we turn to focus on God's saving response to Jonah's destructive attempt to end his life. Jonah has opted for death rather than repentance, but his option is foiled by the God of the sea who appoints a large fish to swallow the drowning prophet. This is not a chance encounter in the deep between man and beast but a merciful intervention by God who orders the great fish to do his work.

Unlike the prophet Elijah, Jonah is not rescued by a fiery chariot; he is not lifted out of the sea by a large bird and brought safely to dry land; he is swallowed by a large fish, a creature at home in the deep, and he is contained there in exile. Jonah will remain in the deep until he accepts his original mission to go to Nineveh and preach God's message.

In the Genesis creation story it is worth noting that the first creatures made by God are the sea monsters: "So God created the great sea monsters and every living creature that moves, of every kind, with which the waters swarm, and every winged bird of every kind. And God saw that it was good" (Genesis 1:21).

The creature that swallows Jonah does not eat him. It is not one of the sea monsters, like the serpent dragon Leviathan, but a large fish who accommodates the terrified prophet for a brief stay.

It's the large fish, or the whale in popular reading, which has dominated this story in people's imagination, making Jonah the most easily recognised prophet in the biblical tradition. God's merciful role in this story is wholly overshadowed by the unlikely coalition between the great fish and Jonah. As the ship carried Jonah from the safety of dry land to the chaos of the storm, so the large fish will carry Jonah from the chaos of the deep to the safety of dry land. In the meantime God will meet Jonah not in a garden like Eden or in the sacred space of a religious sanctuary, but wherever Jonah ends up. Where he ends up is where he will be saved.

Not unlike the Prodigal Son who, after a long journey in flight from where he belonged, ended up in a Gentile's pig-pen where "he came to himself" (Luke 15:17), the prophet Jonah will come to himself in an even more unlikely place as he ends up in the belly of the great fish. Often we do not choose the place where, after detours and deviations, we come home to ourselves: one day we just end up in an unexpected place - where we might feel imprisoned - and the experience forces or invites us to look at ourselves again. The place is irrelevant; it is the moment that is graced. In the memorable lines of T.S. Eliot:

> We shall not cease from exploration
> And the end of all our exploring
> Will be to arrive where we started
> And know the place for the first time.
> Through the unknown, remembered gate
> When the last of earth left to discover
> Is that which was the beginning...[20]

---

[20] T.S. Eliot, *Little Gidding, Four Quartets, The Complete Poems and Plays, 1905–1950* (New York: Harcourt, Brace and World, 1971), 145.

Jonah returns to "that which was the beginning". God is still stubbornly longing for Jonah to find his true self, still hoping that he will abandon the delusion that, to be himself, he must escape the dream of God. What Jonah flees he must embrace: that will be his salvation.

The idea of being swallowed is also used as a metaphor in Hebrew understanding for exile and survival. For example, in a psalm of thanksgiving the people of Israel are encouraged to reflect that the danger they endured in exile and the threat of death were so great – and the deliverance so clearly the work of God that it was proper to remind themselves that they would have been swallowed up alive without the favour of God:

> If it had not been the LORD who was on our side
>
>   – let Israel now say –
>
> if it had not been the LORD who was on our side,
>
>   when our enemies attacked us,
>
> then they would have swallowed us up alive,
>
>   when their anger was kindled against us;
>
> then the flood would have swept us away,
>
>   the torrent would have gone over us;
>
> then over us would have gone
>
>   the raging waters.
>
> (Psalm 124:1-5)

Speaking in the name of Israel, the prophet Jeremiah, using the same imagery, talks of Babylon: "King Nebuchadnezzar of Babylon has devoured me, he has crushed me; he has made me an empty vessel, he has swallowed me like a monster; he has filled his belly with my delicacies, he has spewed me out" (Jeremiah 51:34). With God's help Israel outlives the crushing experience of exile; Jonah will also survive his exile in the belly of the fish, with God's help.

The Jewish philosopher Don Isaac Abarbanel (1437–1508) understood the image of Jonah being in the belly of the fish comparable to a child being in her mother's womb:

> And our eyes see that foetus resides in its mother's belly for nine months without eating, drinking, taking care of his needs, or breathing cold wind, fresh air, from outside. And what would prevent The Eternal from doing so for Jonah for those days?[21]

The psychological imagery of being in the fathomless waters while at the same time being enclosed in a safe protective space seems clear: Jonah is taken into the deep to be born again. This is not so much punishment as a graced opportunity to find new life and new purpose. I have summarised my reading in the following way:

→ Jonah is exiled from land, from ship and from people

→ He is in the depths and out of his depths

→ He is not yet "at himself"

→ He is not in charge

→ Before he passes onwards he must first pass inwards

→ Jonah has to face himself

→ Something in Jonah has to give

→ Something in Jonah has to die

→ The prophet must reclaim his vocation

→ He must reconnect with God.

---

[21] Steven Bob, *Go to Nineveh: Medieval Jewish Commentaries on the Book of Jonah, Translated and Explained* (Oregon: Pickwick, 2013), 88.

Jonah has to revisit and answer the basic questions which haunt him:

→ Who am I? (**identity**)
→ Where am I going? (**direction**)
→ What shapes the way I look at life? (**outlook**)

Jonah is in flight not only from God but from his identity as a prophet. He is afraid for himself. The psychologist and educationalist Jay Lemke has written about how identity and meaning can change in different settings and across different timescales; also how our identities are often built and refashioned in response to what we fear and what we desire:

> We are what we fear, we are what we desire. "Who are we?" is the
>
> basic question of identity. Who by natural gifts and weaknesses?
>
> Who by membership and affiliation? Who by what we have and
>
> what we lack, what we desire and what we fear?[22]

Jonah is in the process of reshaping his identity: he is afraid that Nineveh will destroy his reputation as a prophet whose word proves to be accurate; he desires to be left alone to carve out a new future for himself at the other end of the world. But he has been interrupted in that process, even disabled from seeing it through.

In the infant Church Saul was interrupted and disabled – "Saul got up from the ground, and though his eyes were open, he could see nothing; so they led him by the hand and brought him into Damascus" (Acts 9:8). When Saul was confronted about his destructive mission in persecuting the early followers of Jesus, he went on to change his identity and direction and outlook. For this transformation, he gave himself three years before presenting his reformed self to the leading apostles in Jerusalem and beginning his new mission to the Gentiles (Galatians 1:17-18).

---

[22] Jay Lemke, "Identity, Development and Desire" in *Identity Trouble: Critical Discourse and Contested Identities*, ed. Carmen Caldas-Coulthard and Rick Iedema (London: Palgrave Macmillan, 2010), 27.

When Jonah is stopped in his tracks God sends him on retreat for only three days and three nights. During his retreat there are no lectures, no supervision and no directives: Jonah is on his own. He has to work on himself, direct himself and recollect himself – literally. He has to take the time to collect himself again, as periodically we all have to do when we realise we are hopelessly lost. He has to recollect himself.

Jonah has the opportunity to repent, to change his mind, to begin anew. There is no escape from facing himself and what he has been  commanded to do. His time in the deep offers him the chance to look again at his identity as a prophet, review the direction he has been commanded to take and reassess what defines the choices he makes.

Prayer: Jonah reflects on the past

Then Jonah prayed to the LORD his God
from the belly of the fish, saying,
"I called to the LORD out of my distress,
and he answered me;
out of the belly of Sheol I cried,
and you heard my voice.
You cast me into the deep,
into the heart of the seas,
and the flood surrounded me;
all your waves and your billows
passed over me."

(Jonah 2:1-3)

In the course of his brief exile, something new happens: in the hold of the ship Jonah was passive and reticent, refusing to pray; now in the belly of the great fish he becomes attentive and prayerful. For the first time in the story, we hear the religious figure talking to God. Back in communication with God, Jonah finds a voice for his apprehension and fear, though he does not acknowledge his flight from his mission, the chaos he has brought to all on board the ship, or his failure to repent. If this is a confession, it is entirely opaque.

I don't think we should press Jonah's prayer to equal the prophet's repentance. The puzzling thing about this prayer, like much communication, is what is not said: Jonah neither admits his guilt for fleeing his mission nor does he ask God for forgiveness, although later in the prayer he does promise to honour his vows. Perhaps this is a forewarning of the incompleteness of Jonah's repentance, which will become clearer as his story progresses.

As we move from narrative to poetry we listen to our renegade prophet praying in his distress, imploring God to deliver him from his self-inflicted predicament. We watch Jonah move out of isolation and silence as he reconnects with God. Jonah opens his prayer by acknowledging his current address – in the belly of Sheol, the place of death or, as Hamlet put it, "The undiscover'd country, from whose bourn / No traveller returns".[23] Terence Fretheim comments on the Hebrew concept of death:

> In the Old Testament generally death is never understood simply in medical terms as the cessation of the brain wave or the heart beat. Any form of weakness or misery suffered in life is considered to be the intrusion of death into the sphere of life. Death is thus understood to be more a process than an event.

---

[23] William Shakespeare, *Hamlet*, Act III, scene i.

It is the deterioration or, to use the imagery of the psalm, a "sinking." The greater distress in which a person finds himself the more the reality of death that person experiences.[24]

When King Hezekiah was sick and at the point of death he used the imagery of Sheol and going down to the Pit to reflect what he understood as the finality of his situation:

> I said: In the noontide of my days
> > I must depart;
> I am consigned to the gates of Sheol
> > for the rest of my years.
> I said, I shall not see the LORD
> > in the land of the living;
> I shall look upon mortals no more
> > among the inhabitants of the world…
>
> Surely it was for my welfare
> > that I had great bitterness;
> but you have held back my life
> > from the pit of destruction,
> for you have cast all my sins
> > behind your back.
> For Sheol cannot thank you,
> > death cannot praise you;
> those who go down to the Pit cannot hope
> > for your faithfulness.
> > > (Isaiah 38:10-11. 17-18)

---

[24] Terence E. Fretheim, *The Message of Jonah: a Theological Commentary* (Oregon: Wipf and Stock, 2000), 100.

The outcast Jonah has descended to the place of the dead: only when he is as good as dead is he inclined to pray to the Lord. In that dead place God will meet him and will return him from the Pit. While Jonah bypasses any mention of his culpability, he makes it clear that he understands God to be responsible for his distress: "You cast me into the deep, into the heart of the sea… all your waves and your billows passed over me."

In shifting attention away from himself, Jonah has no problem identifying the Lord as the prime mover in his misfortune: what has happened to him is not mischance, he believes, but has been contrived by God. While theologically correct, this proves a convenient device for switching attention away from Jonah's wrongs to God's mastery. As readers, however, we know that it was Jonah's impulse to flee from God that decided his route towards Tarshish.

That said, what saves Jonah is that his God may be known as the God of Israel, but is not confined to geographical boundaries: as the prophet originally told the sailors, his God is Lord of the heavens and the sea and the land. And the good news is that Jonah knows, even in this deadly place, that the Lord not only hears his voice but answers him in his distress. This is at the heart of the good news of God: no matter how far we sink, we can never descend to a place that is beyond the reach of God's mercy.

Prayer: Jonah describes his situation

Then I said, "I am driven away
from your sight;
how shall I look again
upon your holy temple?"
The waters closed in over me;
the deep surrounded me;
weeds were wrapped around my head
at the roots of the mountains.
I went down to the land
whose bars closed upon me forever;
yet you brought up my life from the Pit,
O LORD my God.

(Jonah 2:4-6)

Surprisingly, Jonah's prayer says nothing about being in the belly of the fish: his prayer is composed from the stock vocabulary of the Psalms, using its two dominant themes of lament and thanksgiving. Jonah speaks of the distress and terror of being cast out from the presence of God – again a peculiar interpretation of events since it was the result of his impulse to flee from the presence of God that has brought him to this place. Originally expressed in the active voice (1:3), his decision to flee is now expressed as his being driven away from God's sight (2:4), told in the passive voice. Jonah takes responsibility for nothing that has happened, content to ascribe his fate entirely to God: this is a useful fiction. His exercise in freedom has culminated in God's judgement which he experiences as anguish at being separated from God.

Jonah wonders if he can look on the holy temple, the unique sanctuary on earth where people journeyed in pilgrimage to the house of God and where sacrifices were made for the sins of the people. These same expectations were expressed by Solomon when he dedicated the temple at its completion, praying that God would attend all those who prayed towards the temple:

> LORD my God, heeding the cry and the prayer that your servant prays to you today; that your eyes may be open night and day toward this house, the place of which you said, "My name shall be there", that you may heed the prayer that your servant prays toward this place. Hear the plea of your servant and of your people Israel when they pray towards this place; O hear in heaven your dwelling place; heed and forgive.
>
> (1 Kings 8:28-30)

In his prayer Jonah returns to describing his ordeal. Throughout his appeal the wayward prophet devotes more time to describing his personal torment than he does acknowledging his deliverance by God. Clearly Jonah remains more fascinated by his own story than that of his redeemer, not unlike the Pharisee, in Jesus' parable, whose ego dominates centre-stage during his prayer, edging God to the fringes (Luke 18:9-14).

Jonah returns to describing his experience of drowning: the waters closed over him; the deep surrounded him; he descends to the bottom of the mountains where weeds wrap around his head. When Jonah descends to the bottom of the sea, it looks like the deep has embraced him as its own, forever excluding him from the kindness of God. Jonah descends to the root of the mountains – referring to the popular Hebrew understanding that the earth was supported by two subterranean mountains.[25] These mountains flanked the entrance to Sheol: Jonah has reached the deepest part of the deep; he has hit rock bottom. The bars (gates) of Sheol have closed in upon him.

In descending to the base of these mountains, which mark the threshold of the underworld, the imperilled Jonah is the farthest he can be from the Lord's presence represented by the temple, which was built on top of the sacred mountain in Jerusalem. I think this contrast is stunning – between the mountaintop, grounded on land, where the Lord's presence abides and the deep base of these mountains, rooted at the bottom of the deep, where the drowning prophet faces annihilation.

---

[25] See Michael D. Coogan, *A Brief Introduction to the Old Testament: The Hebrew Bible in its Context* (New York: Oxford University Press, 2011), 29.

Yet Jonah is not abandoned to the grasp of the deep: he experiences the unexpected salvation of God who brings him out of the Pit, clutching him from the threshold of death. God reverses Jonah's descent and brings him back up from Sheol. Jonah's brief recognition of divine deliverance is the prophet's only mention of God's salvation in the whole book.

In Shakespeare's play *The Tempest*, words from Ariel's song might summarise Jonah's change in the deep:

> Nothing of him that does fade,
>
> But doth suffer a sea-change
>
> Into something rich and strange.[26]

---

[26] William Shakespeare, *The Tempest*, Act I, scene ii.

Prayer: Jonah remembers the Lord

As my life was ebbing away
I remembered the LORD;
and my prayer came to you,
into your holy temple
Those who worship vain idols
forsake their true loyalty.

(Jonah 2:7-8)

Jonah moves away from his brief acknowledgement of God's deliverance to focus on the power of his personal prayer. Just in time, with his life ebbing away, Jonah states that his memory of the Lord saves him from total despair and destruction. I think, however, that Jonah's interpretation seems wholly lopsided: it is not Jonah's remembrance of the Lord but the Lord's remembrance of Jonah that has saved him. Jonah remains stubbornly centred on himself as the principal actor in the drama, as if somehow he is the architect of his own salvation.

As the prophet moves into prayer, his earlier hope is realised that it would reach into the holy temple. Jonah could hardly be farther away from the temple than he is now, either in distance or moral uprightness, yet the God who resides in the temple is not limited in his authority to that sacred space or to the land of Israel; neither is he restricted to paying heed only to the upright. Jonah's prayer mirrors that of King David:

> For the waves of death encompassed me,
>> the torrents of perdition assailed me;
> the cords of Sheol entangled me,
>> the snares of death confronted me.
>
> In my distress I called upon the LORD;
>> to my God I called.
> From his temple he heard my voice,
>> and my cry came to his ears.
>
> (2 Samuel 22: 5-7)

God brings both David and Jonah out of Sheol. As God listens to his erratic prophet and to the pleas of the sailors, so he will surely listen to the cries of the sinful people of Nineveh. This is good news indeed: no matter how far we wander from the right path, no matter if we ignore God completely and follow our own designs, God remains reachable by prayer.

Jonah goes on to compare himself favourably to those who worship vain idols and who "forsake their true loyalty." This flattery sounds puzzling since it describes exactly what Jonah has done in making an idol of his own theological outlook in seeking to limit the reach of God's mercy, a view that has led him to forsake his loyalty to God and his vocation. This "son of faithfulness" has belied his name. It is Jonah's loyalty to God that is the issue, not the loyalty of the Gentiles. In the boat the idol-worshipping sailors abandoned their false gods and put their trust in Jonah's God – as will the Ninevites when they hear the word of the Lord. As Daniel Timmer observes:

> This invective against Gentiles, therefore, condemns Jonah with delicious irony while reminding us that God has in fact delivered the Gentile sailors in more senses than one. The irony only increases when Jonah promises that he will sacrifice to Yahweh with a thankful voice and pay his vows, the very two actions that have already demonstrated the sailors' reverence for Yahweh in 1:16.[27]

---

[27] Daniel C. Timmer, *A Gracious and Compassionate God: Mission, salvation and spirituality in the book of Jonah*, New Studies in Biblical Theology 26 (Illinois: Inter-Varsity Press, 2011), 88.

Prayer: Jonah makes his promises

But I with the voice of thanksgiving
will sacrifice to you;
what I have vowed I will pay.
Deliverance belongs to the LORD!

(Jonah 2:9)

It seems strange that at this point Jonah does not promise to fulfil the original commission he received from God, to go to the pagan city of Nineveh and preach the word of the Lord. Instead Jonah promises to offer cultic sacrifices - as if liturgical propriety is what God seeks from him, as if the act of presenting burnt offerings will remedy everything that Jonah has done and restore the early relationship. Rather than looking for acts of piety from Jonah, God is looking for a fundamental change of heart: we will learn that God will continue to look for that change of heart even to the last sentence of the book of Jonah.

The prayer of Jonah concludes with the exclamation, "Deliverance belongs to the LORD!" Although a perfect theological maxim, Jonah will be unable to sign up to this when God does exactly that in delivering the sinful people of Nineveh. This will be the Lord's choice, certainly not Jonah's: the prophet will continue to look for judgement and punishment. While Jonah's profession of faith is exemplary regarding his own destiny, it will prove too much when extended to his favourite enemy.

While Jonah is delighted to be the beneficiary of God's mercy, that same mercy must, in his understanding, be subject to his approval before being extended to others. (Sometimes we should thank God that it is God who is God, not some of his acolytes who would veto God's indiscriminate mercy.) In spite of his creedal  affirmation Jonah will remain ambivalent to the end, rendering his bold assertion of faith, it has to be said, somewhat hollow. What Jonah now affirms in faith he will deny in Nineveh.

Back on dry land

Then the LORD spoke to the fish, and it spewed Jonah out upon the dry land.

(Jonah 2:10)

Jonah worshipped false idols – his theological outlook, his fear, his self-image, his reputation – and so abandoned his true loyalty to God. He has professed to fulfil his vows to the Lord, none of which is specified.

When Jonah makes his pious profession, the large fish vomits Jonah out of its system onto dry land. Holbert believes that the big fish is sick to the stomach of Jonah's hypocrisy, commenting: "It is no wonder that immediately after Jonah shouts, 'Deliverance belongs to Yahweh!' the big fish throws up!"[28]

Making the big fish theologically sensitive might be stretching the text too far; the reading states that it is God who commands the fish to deposit Jonah on the land. This done, the runaway to sea is back on *terra firma*, back in his element. The hunt is over; the prophet is reclaimed and returned; the original mission will have a second start. We will now follow the turbulent prophet as he agrees to go in the direction God originally commanded.

---

[28] J.C. Holbert, "Deliverance belongs to Yahweh!: Satire in the Book of Jonah" in *Journal for the Study of the Old Testament* 21(Sheffield: Sheffield Academic Press, 1981), 59-81.

But questions remain outstanding: will Jonah manage to come to terms with what he has experienced? Will he learn that the God who has heaped mercy on the Gentile sailors and on his elected prophet is, truly, a God of deliverance? That the God who has forgiven him and raised him from Sheol is capable of forgiving foreigners and raising them from the pit of their sinfulness?

That story remains to be told.

The second mission

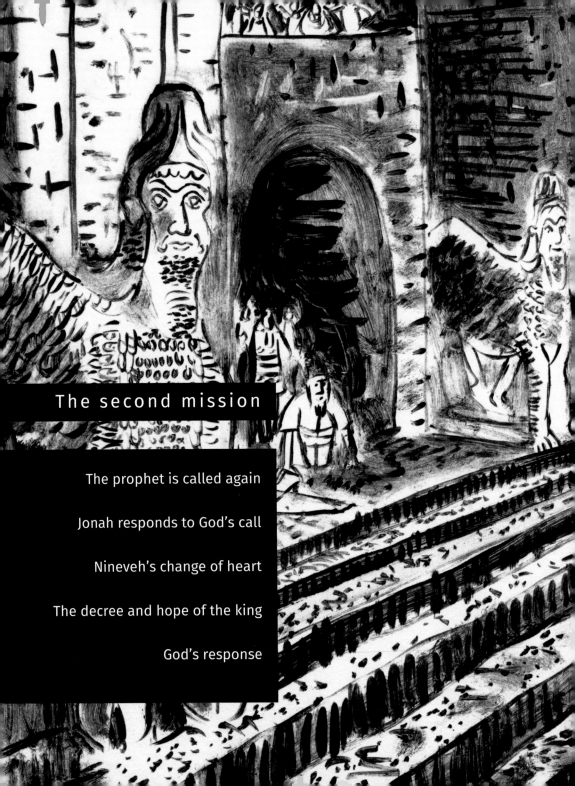

The second mission

The prophet is called again

Jonah responds to God's call

Nineveh's change of heart

The decree and hope of the king

God's response

The prophet is called again

The word of the LORD came to Jonah a second time, saying, "Get up, go to Nineveh, that great city, and proclaim to it the message that I tell you." So Jonah set out and went to Nineveh, according to the word of the LORD.

(Jonah 3:1-3a)

We return now to the beginning of the story, with the repeat of Jonah's original commission. Between the two assignments Jonah has travelled far, both geographically and psychologically. As the runaway prophet opted for distance, God chose to take him into custody; as Jonah headed outwards, God elected he move inwards. Bound for the freedom of a faraway place in Tarshish, Jonah was forced to come up against a more intimate destination, himself. No prophet has been so forcefully compelled to rethink his identity, his direction and his outlook.

Jonah is the only biblical prophet who needed to be given his assignment twice, although in the New Testament Simon son of Jonah will also be called a second time (John 21:15-19). Although Jonah is called again, his benevolent God does not rebuke him for his earlier disobedience or for the disaster that followed the first call; neither does God remind Jonah of his deliverance from Sheol or the vows he has recently professed. No warning is issued if he does not obey. The past is now forgotten; an earlier challenge is refreshed; a new opportunity awaits. God's mercy is never fixated on past failures; rather, God's forbearance focuses ahead, kindly presuming that Jonah will honour his call and not choose flight again.

Surprisingly, we do not hear the exact words of the Lord's message to Nineveh: there is no formula, "Thus says the Lord to the people of Nineveh…" In the first call Jonah was commissioned: *"Go at once to Nineveh, that great city, and cry out against it; for their wickedness has come up before me"* (1:2). Now Jonah's charge appears noticeably softened: *"Get up, go to Nineveh, that great city, and proclaim to it the message that I tell you"* (3:2). The preposition "against" Nineveh is replaced by "to" Nineveh. Commenting on the Hebrew text Jack Sasson writes:

> The sentence duplicates 1:2 in vocabulary until it reaches the preposition 'el, which here replaces 'al… The first time around Nineveh is simply being served with a death warrant… In this case Nineveh will receive a special message from Israel's god.[29]

---

[29] Jack M. Sasson, *Jonah*, The Anchor Yale Bible 24b (New Haven: Yale University Press, 1995), 226.

In this second commission the tone of the imperative seems different, more hopeful, moving away from the prospect of the Ninevites just hearing God's final and irrevocable judgement to their being challenged by God's message, thus inviting their response. Their fate is not sealed; now the future looks more open than it did.

What will Jonah do this time? If Jonah responds by word, we are not told; neither are we given access to what he thinks or feels at this point. The text is silent; the suspense remains. Replying to the first commission, Jonah got up to flee; he now gets up and goes. We are simply informed what Jonah does: that he allows the word of God to direct his path as he obediently sets out for Nineveh. Jonah is on the right road.

Jonah now acts out of his identity as a prophet of the Lord; he follows the direction he has been commanded to take; he will allow the word of God to shape the outlook he will share with the Ninevites. But as

we will soon learn his negative attitude to this mission will remain unchanged. It has to be acknowledged that he performs well according to the script he has been given; his heart, however, is not in it.

Jonah responds to God's call

Now Nineveh was an exceedingly large city, a three days' walk across. Jonah began to go into the city, going a day's walk. And he cried out, "Forty days more, and Nineveh shall be overthrown!"

(Jonah 3:3b-4)

For the third time in the narrative Nineveh is described as a great city. The description that it would take three days to cross the city is possibly an exaggeration, one that probably serves to underline the importance of the city rather than its size. At that time the total area of Nineveh comprised about seven square kilometres.

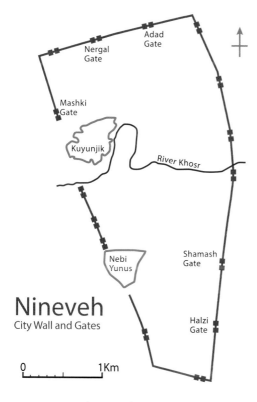

Nineveh
City Wall and Gates

0   1Km

As you can see from the map opposite, fifteen great gates guarded the city and allowed access (the named gates in the map have all been excavated).[30] The ruin of Kuyunjik has been extensively excavated uncovering a number of palaces and temples. The site Nebi Yunus marks the traditional tomb of Jonah which was blown up by Islamic State in July 2014. An elaborate system of eighteen canals brought water from the hills to Nineveh, and some sections of an elaborately constructed aqueduct were discovered about 65 kilometres distant. The enclosed area had more than 150,000 inhabitants, making it the largest city in the ancient world.

Often the gates of Assyrian cities were protected by huge stone carvings of the bodies of winged animals, usually bulls or lions, with the head of a bearded male. Known as lamassu (protective deities) they guarded the city gates against demonic forces, assuring protection to the comings and goings of the king and the citizens. No doubt stone carvings of these protective gods, such as the Assyrian examples (see next page), now in the Louvre, were the first thing Jonah saw when he approached Nineveh.[31]

---

[30] Licensed under CC BY-SA 3.0

[31] Licensed under CC BY-SA 3.0

The great Gentile city of Nineveh is now going to welcome an unusual guest in this Israelite prophet from the Galilean countryside. Jonah's journey has ended, his destination now reached "according to the word of the LORD." The mission takes over as Jonah crosses national and theological boundaries to preach to a pagan people. He goes into the great city and his announcement seems, at first reading, only to mean one thing: that all the people, without exception, will be destroyed in forty days. There is neither explanation of why this is going to happen nor details of what form the punishment will take. Also the standard prophetic formula "Thus says the Lord" is not offered to give formal validation to the prophet's speech, indicating the divine origin of the message.

The time element, "forty days more", takes precedence, emphasising the amount of time Nineveh's inhabitants have to respond before the city will be overturned. In the biblical narrative the number forty usually signals a time of trial that leads to renewal, dominant among the examples being the forty years the chosen people endured in the wilderness before entering the Promised Land. In the story of Noah the waters covered the earth for forty days (Genesis 7:17); Moses remained on the mountain with God for forty days (Exodus 24:18); Ezekiel was assigned to bear the punishment of Judah for forty days (Ezekiel 4:6). The forty days given to the people of Nineveh will, no doubt, prove to be an equally testing time for the prophet Jonah.

There appears neither ambiguity nor subtlety about Jonah's message; but perhaps there is. As Kevin Youngblood comments:

> The verb "overturn" (hāpak) recalls the destruction of Sodom and Gomorrah as the historical precedent for God's response to extreme wickedness and, by association with this context, clearly conveys the possibility of annihilation (Genesis 19:21, 25, 29).

> The verb "overturn" (hāpak), however, also carries the sense "to change/reform," which opens the possibility of the alternate interpretation: "Forty days until Nineveh is reformed." It is possible that Jonah's oracle contained ambiguity. Like the forty-day time frame, the verb portending Nineveh's destruction suggested two possible fates: destruction by physical overturning of the city, or reformation by an ethical overturning of the citizens' behaviour.[32]

This nuanced interpretation allows for what actually happens: the people of Nineveh will indeed turn around, changing their mind and their behaviour. If Jonah was certain that his message was wholly unambiguous, holding out no hope for the city of Nineveh, why would he have fled in the first instance? Jonah, more than anything, wants the destruction of his country's oppressor, Assyria, and it would surely have pleased him that he was the chosen Israelite to announce the oracle of the annihilation of its capital city. That would have attracted him, not repelled him. Given his actions, Jonah seems to believe in the ambiguity his message carries: hence his flight from the presence of God. Jonah's horror will soon be revealed, when his feared enemy responds to God's message and enjoys the strangeness of God's mercy.

---

[32] Kevin J. Youngblood, *Jonah: God's Scandalous Mercy* (Grand Rapids: Zondervan, 2013), 134.

Nineveh's change of heart

And the people of Nineveh believed God; they proclaimed a fast, and everyone, great and small, put on sackcloth. When the news reached the king of Nineveh, he rose from his throne, removed his robe, covered himself with sackcloth, and sat in ashes.

(Jonah 3:5-6)

Attention now shifts away from Jonah, who plays no part in this critical scene, to focus on the prompt and dramatic response of the people and the king of Nineveh. The people do not assemble in the city square to discuss the prophet's message; they do not break up into groups to discuss how they might respond; they do not arrange a city-wide poll, calculating the people's opinion. The common people respond instinctively and immediately, believing that this message is not irrevocable, which will prove to be right. Importantly they do not resign themselves to fatalism or abandon themselves to self-pity: they believe that they can do something to make a difference; they believe in the wonder of "perhaps".

The king and his court will follow the example of the people: their combined generous response to the word of God stands in dramatic contrast to the initial disobedience of Jonah. The text does not say that the people of Nineveh believed Jonah but that they believed God. The word that Jonah spoke is understood by the people to be the authoritative word of God; and there is nothing shallow or half-hearted about their response.

Jesus will use the Ninevites' generous response to make a stark contrast with the obduracy of his own listeners:

> The people of Nineveh will rise up at the judgment with this generation and condemn it, because they repented at the proclamation of Jonah, and see, something greater than Jonah is here!
>
> (Matthew 12:41)

No prophet and no preacher in history has ever enjoyed such a generous response as Jonah receives from the whole people of Nineveh: the message he preaches prompts a ready and radical response.

Interestingly, the people do not wait for the king's lead but react before he does, proclaiming a fast and putting on sackcloth. And when the king does hear the same message, independently of Jonah, his answer is immediate as he moves from sitting on his throne to sitting in an ash heap in a dramatic sign of repentance. The king's verbs are telling:

> he **rises** from his throne;
>
> he **removes** his robe;
>
> he **covers** himself with sackcloth;
>
> he **sits** in ashes.

This image of a humbled and repentant king is a long way from the images that decorated the king's apartments in the Northern Palace at Nineveh, exhibiting lion-hunt scenes carved in alabaster bas-reliefs. Among the finest, now in the British Museum, the king's sovereignty and skill are shown as he stands calm and upright while he despatches the attacking lion with his sword (opposite). Behind the king, his attendant remains strangely aloof from the danger, wholly confident in his master's ability to frustrate any threat. In this image the absolute power of the king is demonstrated by his assured victory over the threat of the wild. Scenes like this were also read as a summary of Assyria's brutal military dominance: nothing, not even the strongest savage beasts, could threaten the majesty that reigned in Nineveh.

In the book of Jonah, however, the king of Nineveh appears not as invincible and assured but as vulnerable and contrite. The word of God, not the wild beasts, has threatened the threshold of his sanctuary. When he removes his luxurious royal robes that signalled his exclusive status as king and dons sackcloth, the king makes himself indistinguishable from all his people. Hierarchy has no place in collective repentance which disassembles power structures: everyone in the city is now dressed alike; everyone shares the same humble attitude.

Before God everyone is equal, something Jonah has yet to learn.

Before the king decrees national penitence, he demonstrates the proper response by his own actions; indeed he goes further than his people and sits in an ash heap. It is a measure of his continuing authority, however, that he is able to issue a decree from such an unlikely address.

The decree and hope of the king

Then he had a proclamation made in Nineveh: "By the decree of the king and his nobles: No human being or animal, no herd or flock, shall taste anything. They shall not feed, nor shall they drink water. Human beings and animals shall be covered with sackcloth, and they shall cry mightily to God. All shall turn from their evil ways and from the violence that is in their hands. Who knows? God may relent and change his mind; he may turn from his fierce anger, so that we do not perish."

(Jonah 3:7-9)

The vast gulf between the Assyrian aristocracy and the common people is bridged in their common cause of repentance. The ready and wholehearted response of the people of Nineveh is now promulgated by the king as government policy. Somewhat comically the king then orders that not only the people but the flocks and herds must fast and go without water, underlining the totality of Nineveh's response. As the city's livestock these animals are a key part of the prosperity of Nineveh; they must, therefore, play their part in the city's lively ritual of repentance. As the large fish was an instrument of God's salvation, so Nineveh's animals will be a model of compliance to the will of God.[33] In an agrarian society there is solidarity between humans and animals. Reflecting on that bond the writer of Ecclesiastes reflects:

> For the fate of humans and the fate of animals is the same; as one dies, so dies the other. They all have the same breath, and humans have no advantage over the animals; for all is vanity. All go to one place; all are from the dust, and all turn to dust again. Who knows whether the human spirit goes upward and the spirit of animals goes downward to the earth?
>
> (Ecclesiastes 3:19-21)

The king orders the people and the animals to cry mightily to God, in sounds of lamentation. The whole city is howling, keening, making a mighty dirge. But this shared ritual is not just about making gestures – changing into a dull wardrobe of goat's hair, fasting, going without water and lamenting – but about dramatically changing course. More important than the outward gestures, the king commands that every living thing turns away from evil and from violence. This pagan king of Nineveh knows that the habitual pattern of wickedness and brutality in his city has to be broken if the people are to be saved.

---

[33] Yael Shemesh, "The Function and Status of Animals in the Book of Jonah" in *Journal of Hebrew Scriptures* 10 (2010), 5-8.

Everyone in Nineveh pays attention, including the animals. All not only hear the word of God but do it. The king entertains the wondrous thought: "Who knows? God may relent and change his mind; he may turn from his fierce anger, so that we do not perish." The king cannot be certain, of course, but he entertains the fond hope that God might pay attention to how he, the nobles, and all the people have responded to God's word. As Terence Fretheim comments:

> Who knows? This statement by the captain reflects a very sophisticated understanding of God and his activity in the world... That this understanding should be found only on the lips of the heathen (captain, sailors, king) is one of the ironic features of the book. It is the heathen rather than Jonah who have such extraordinary insight into the sovereign freedom of God. They, in fact, articulate what Jonah refuses to allow in his God: God acts as it pleases him, which may or may not conform to human expectations.[34]

Who knows? Who knows? The king shares the belief expressed at the end of Jonah's prayer: "Deliverance belongs to the LORD!" (2:9). Without being instructed to think or hope like this by the prophet Jonah, this extraordinary king turns prophet himself, his hope exactly mirroring the prophet Joel when he instructs Israel:

---

[34] Terence Fretheim, *The Message of Jonah*, 112-113.

Yet even now, says the LORD,

    return to me with all your heart,

with fasting, with weeping, and with mourning;

    rend your hearts and not your clothing.

Return to the LORD, your God,

    for he is gracious and merciful,

slow to anger, and abounding in steadfast love,

    and relents from punishing.

Who knows whether he will not turn and relent,

    and leave a blessing behind him?

                               (Joel 2:12-14)

Again there is the question, "Who knows?" Paradoxically, the shared hope of the king of Nineveh and the prophet Joel is one that is shared silently, not as hope but as dread, by Jonah. This we will soon learn (Jonah 4:2).

God's response

When God saw what they did, how they turned from their evil ways, God changed his mind about the calamity that he had said he would bring upon them; and he did not do it.

(Jonah 3:10)

The narrative moves from the king's plea for mercy to God's response to the people's repentance. The king's question, "Who knows?" now finds a sure answer. As the king hoped, God does indeed notice the response of the people. He is not so much impressed by the street theatre of sackcloth and ashes as by the fact that the people of Nineveh have all turned from their evil ways.

They have indeed changed and God is moved by their resolution: in turning towards the people of Nineveh in compassion, God now turns away from his intention to destroy the great city.

God's compassion outshines his anger; his mercy eclipses his disappointment; his stubborn love overshadows their past sins. The power of God's abiding mercy is that the past is emptied of its power and is obliterated; it is not simply biding its time in the shadows for the opportune moment to appear and accuse. God's mercy dissolves past wrongs and opens the way to a fresh future. That is the unique and liberating power of God's forgiveness.

As the captain and the sailors retired from the narrative after experiencing the kindness of God, so now the king and the people of Nineveh withdraw from the story after being graced by God's tender mercy.

The people of Nineveh have repented: however important this turning-point is, if that were the point of this book, it would end here. The challenge of this story, however, is not the repentance of Nineveh but the repentance of Jonah. That story remains outstanding.

The unfinished ending

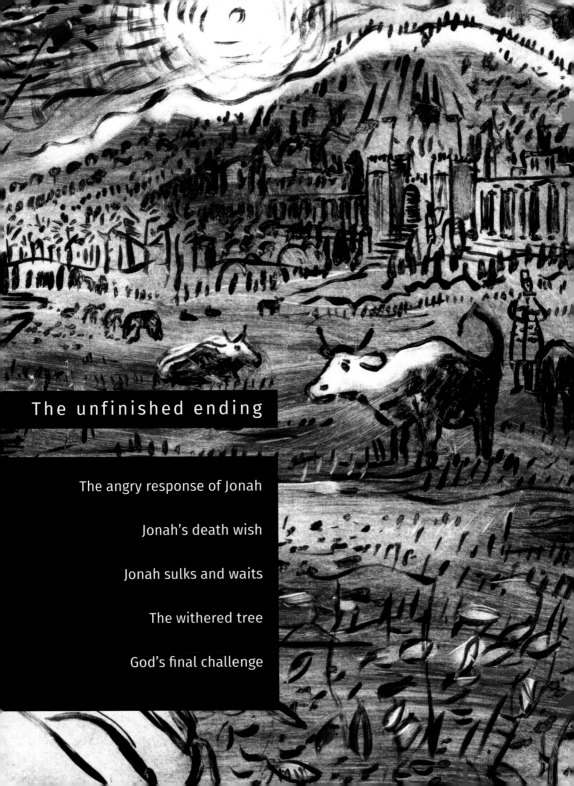

The unfinished ending

The angry response of Jonah

Jonah's death wish

Jonah sulks and waits

The withered tree

God's final challenge

The angry response of Jonah

But this was very displeasing to Jonah, and he became angry. He prayed to the LORD and said, "O LORD! Is not this what I said while I was still in my own country? That is why I fled to Tarshish at the beginning; for I knew that you are a gracious God and merciful, slow to anger, and abounding in steadfast love, and ready to relent from punishing."

(Jonah 4:1-2)

As the king, the nobles and the people of Nineveh recede from view following their conversion and God's merciful response, the story now focuses on the relationship between God and his reluctant prophet. Clearly this is Jonah's story. The destruction that Jonah announced would surely befall the whole city of Nineveh has not happened; Jonah's prophecy has not been fulfilled; his greatest fear has now been realised – God has relented and the pagan people have been spared God's wrath.

A reason for rejoicing, surely: a city, its entire population and all the animals saved? Jonah's judgement about God's clemency, however, is entirely negative and he moves from frustration to open anger, furious that God has not destroyed the enemy city. Although he describes God as "slow to anger", Jonah feels no obligation either to imitate his Lord or to live up to the meaning of his name: "a dove".

In Jonah's estimation, God's mercy has been offered to the most unlikely and undeserving people. He has yet to learn that no one deserves mercy. For me, that point is well made in a story told of a young French soldier who deserted Napoleon's army but who, within a matter of hours, was caught by his own troops. To discourage soldiers from abandoning their posts the penalty for desertion was death. The young soldier's mother, who was Napoleon's cook, heard what had happened and went to plead with Napoleon to spare the life of her son. Napoleon heard her plea but pointed out that because of the serious nature of the crime her son had committed he clearly did not deserve mercy.

"I know he doesn't deserve mercy," the mother answered. "It would not be mercy if he deserved it."

That is the point about mercy: nobody deserves it. Everyone deserves true justice; mercy, on the other hand, is sheer gift. Mercy cancels out wrongs and transgressions – not because a sparkling defence has been found or excusing causes have been skilfully argued – but because that is the free response of the God who is grieved. Mercy does not suggest that the guilty are not guilty; it recognises the wrongdoing but does not demand satisfaction for the wrong. In all this, mercy reflects the utter graciousness of the God who has been wronged.

Jonah has a problem with the nature of mercy. In his mounting anger Jonah castigates God for being God. He has crossed the geographical boundary by travelling into Nineveh; he has yet to cross the theological boundary by struggling to understand and submit to the wondrous ways of God. In Jonah's understanding God's preferences should mirror his own; there is no room for God's total otherness. In Jonah's theological outlook, unlike that of the captain of the ship and the king of Nineveh, there is no room for wondering "Perhaps?" or "Who knows?" Yet these two questions go beyond the confines of the present moment and allow God to be God, acknowledging the real possibility of good news; these two questions provide ground for hope that nothing is settled, nothing is sealed. The future is not contained inside the present moment.

The questions of the sailors and the king, rather than the fixed anger of Jonah, point towards new hope. Hope is not an interior resource that needs nothing but itself; if hope exists within us, it is because we believe that there is help outside of us. Hope is not absolute. As William Lynch observed: "The fact is that hope is a relative idea. It is always relative to the idea of help. It seeks help. It depends. It looks to the outside world."[35]

Like the sailors and the people of Nineveh, hope is dedicated to imagining a way out or a way forward; it imagines the possible; it does not stay within the constrictions of the present moment. If people feel totally stuck in a situation, they can lose a sense of the possible and so have no energy to hope. They stare at the present, obsessed with the detail and clutter of failure, and lose belief in the possibility of getting anywhere precisely because they feel trapped in a structure of hopelessness.

---

[35] William F. Lynch, *Images of Hope: Imagination as Healer of the Hopeless* (New York: Mentor-Omega, 1966), 23.

Imagination is an essential characteristic of hope; imagination allows us to go beyond the present moment and envisage change; it refuses to stay within the limitations of the here and now. William Lynch observes the movement when he writes:

> For one of the permanent meanings of imagination has been that it is the gift that envisions what cannot yet be seen, the gift that constantly proposes to itself that the boundaries of the possible are wider than they seem. Imagination, if it is in prison and has tried every exit, does not panic or move into apathy but sits down to try to envision another way out. It is always slow to admit that all the facts are in, that all the doors have been tried, and that it is defeated. It is not so much that it has vision as that it is able to wait, to wait for the moment of vision which is not yet here, for a door that is not locked. It is not overcome by the absoluteness of the present moment.[36]

Hopelessness, on the other hand, does not go beyond the limits of what is presently happening because it does not believe in the possibility of help; it has no energy to imagine, unable as it is to envisage anything that could be done to manage or improve the situation; it cannot think of anything worth planning or doing. Hence the rejoinder: "There's no point." Hopelessness is marked by non-participation and non-involvement in life: the hopeless want to be left alone, as Jonah does, to retreat into the absence of concern.

Those who hope wait inside their hope, which is an act of protest against the tyranny of the instant. The present moment is not an absolute atomic reality. Investing in "Perhaps?" and "Who knows?" deprives the painful present from being utterly preoccupying in its power; it finds a larger context of understanding and a bigger frame of reference.

[36] Lynch, *Images of Hope*, 27.

Jonah's theology regarding mercy for the Ninevites has no room for the question "Perhaps?" Jonah's angry outlook and God's gracious perspective are at loggerheads, with no foreseeable resolution in sight. Jonah does indeed believe that God is merciful, but our Israelite prophet cannot accept that that same mercy should be extended to the pagan Ninevites. Mercy should be confined to himself and his own people; it is a restricted privilege, not for foreign export. Jonah demands justice and punishment for the Ninevites' past evil ways, not magnanimity following their recent repentance.

The repentance of the Ninevites will stand as an accusation against Israel's lack of it, as it will continue to do in Jesus' day and, indeed, for every other day for every other society. God held out judgement and mercy to the people of Nineveh, and mercy prevailed; Jonah holds fast to judgement, dismissing mercy as wholly unfitting for those he judges to live beyond the boundaries of religious and social approval. It has to be acknowledged that the original readers of this book would agree with Jonah; it might be acknowledged that most of us might be sympathetic to Jonah's view, although our target audience might be different. Jonah, like most of us, if not all, wants God to reflect his own outlook.

In *The Merchant of Venice* William Shakespeare's character Portia, addressing the complainant Shylock who demands justice from the court, summarises the peril of insisting on justice rather than pleading for mercy:

> Though justice be thy plea, consider this,
>
> That, in the course of justice, none of us
>
> Should see salvation: we do pray for mercy;
>
> And that same prayer doth teach us all to render
>
> The deeds of mercy.[37]

---

[37] William Shakespeare, *The Merchant of Venice*, Act IV, scene i.

As Shakespeare noted, at the bar of justice none of us should see salvation. None. Mercy, the playwright argues, should be contagious: once the unearned grace is experienced, it should be extended to others. One cannot hope for mercy for oneself and then deny it to others. As it states eloquently in Sirach 28:2-4:

> Forgive your neighbour the wrong he has done,
>> and then your sins will be pardoned when you pray.
> Does anyone harbour anger against another,
>> and expect healing from the Lord?
> If one has no mercy toward another like himself,
>> can he then seek pardon for his own sins?

In the Gospel of Luke, Jesus announces: "I tell you, there will be more joy in heaven over one sinner who repents than over ninety-nine righteous persons who need no repentance" (Luke 15:7). The repentance of the whole city of Nineveh brings no joy to Jonah. We might have thought he was a reformed character as he moved away from his forced confinement in the great fish to follow God's direction to Nineveh; instead, he has crawled back into his angry bubble of self-centeredness.

Jonah proceeds to press his case, arguing with God. As Jonah suspected all along, God has a controlling habit of forgiveness. He says to God: "I knew that you are a gracious God and merciful, slow to anger, and abounding in steadfast love, and ready to relent from punishing." That was why he fled. Jonah accuses God of being merciful, condemning God's indiscriminate compassion.

Paradoxically, Jonah's accusation is our Gospel.

Jonah's insistent pride remains intact in spite of all that he has endured, not least in spite of God having saved him from death by drowning.

Rabbi Shlomo Yitzhaki (1040–1105) interprets his understanding of Jonah 4:2: "I knew that if they returned to You in repentance You would not destroy them and I would become a liar in their eyes."[38] Jonah's own understanding still remains in primary place; God's way of acting holds no sway against what is central in Jonah's life – preoccupation with himself, with his reputation in the eyes of others, with his own outlook. Jonah's inflated sense of his own identity looks close to idolatry. Although not discussing Jonah, the theologian and psychologist Terry Cooper's discussion of sin and pride throws some light on Jonah's problem:

> Many of us interested in both Christian theology and psychology often come to a crossroads in our journey. Frequently our theological understanding of the dynamics of sin is greatly influenced by the Augustinian tradition with its accent on pride as the primary human problem. This tradition asserts that as we refuse to trust God, we substitute ourselves as the centre of our existence. Ignoring our Creator, we egocentrically attempt to control reality. We think more highly of ourselves that is warranted. From this angle, grandiosity is the self's nagging tendency… Humility and care for others are the important qualities lacking in our self-preoccupation and self-elevations. Within the Judeo-Christian tradition, this self-centredness is a form of idolatry identified as sin.[39]

---

[38] Steven Bob, *Medieval Commentaries on the Book of Jonah*, 15.

[39] Terry D. Cooper, *Sin, Pride and Self-Acceptance: the Problem of Identity in Theology & Psychology* (Illinois: IVP Academic, 2003), 7.

Certainly Jonah has shown neither humility nor care for others. Jonah believes that he should have the last word about the fate of Nineveh because his picture of the world is the orthodox one. He overvalues himself and as a consequence distrusts God. Jonah's earlier rebellion against God is now repeated in his exaggerated sense of self and his belief that his own outlook should eclipse that of God's. Jonah has learned nothing; he is back where he started, running away from the strangeness of this merciful God.

Jonah believes that his identity and integrity as a prophet has been violated by God's act of mercy to the Ninevites. Yes, Jonah has been made to look reckless, publicly assuring a fate for Nineveh that did not happen. But our prophet has to learn that the point of prophecy is not accuracy, but repentance. The point of preaching is not to be proved right in the public arena but to challenge people to think again, to invest in the "Perhaps?" and the "Who knows?"; the point of preaching is to hold out the prospect of change, to introduce the wonder of God's plentiful redemption. Yes, Jonah has lost his face and now feels foolish, but his foolishness is less important than people's salvation.

Our minor prophet has to learn what the Major Prophets all knew: that sometimes you have to look foolish in the service of God's word; sometimes you have to forget yourself and your own hunger for respectability so that the power of the Lord's word can be heard and felt. Sometimes you have to dump your carefully crafted self-image so that others might know the power of salvation. Sometimes you have to go beyond your enclosed world of judgement and stubborn self-righteousness and reach out in compassion to others, rejoicing with them in their liberation.

As we enter the last act of this drama Jonah's challenge remains outstanding:

→ His **identity** and vocation as a prophet of God

→ His **direction** to follow God's will

→ His **outlook** to be formed by God's choices.

Jonah's death wish

"And now, O LORD, please take my life from me, for it is better for me to die than to live."

(Jonah 4:3)

Jonah now asks God to take his life, again preferring death to following God's plan. Given that he prefers death, Jonah has nothing to lose in continuing to argue with God and insists on the probity of his own theological outlook. He now appears somewhat childish and petulant: if he cannot have his way, there is no more purpose in living.

Jonah really does have a death wish; he has been put to shame, so he returns to his favourite obsession: himself and his own reputation. He wants Nineveh destroyed only because he predicted it. He wants to be right, and he is ready to see an entire city destroyed to be proved so - even if he will be the only human being to witness this. Who would applaud the prophet? His arrogance is overwhelming. Jonah lives in a small world bounded on the north and the south and the east and the west by Jonah.

It might be worth noting that Jonah's wish for death is not unlike that of the prophet Elijah, but there is a noticeable difference:

But he himself went a day's journey into the wilderness, and
came and sat down under a solitary broom tree. He asked that
he might die: "It is enough; now, O Lᴏʀᴅ, take away my life, for
I am no better than my ancestors."

(1 Kings 19:4)

Elijah's death wish emerges from despair at his failure to convert the
idolatrous Israelites; Jonah's death wish emerges from anger at his
success in converting the pagan Ninevites. Jonah has remained angry
because God has proved, as the prophet protested, that one of the
divine characteristics is being slow to anger. Jonah seeks the end of his
life because God has restored the lives of the people of Nineveh. Are
God and Jonah completely irreconcilable?

Jonah sulks and waits

And the LORD said, "Is it right for you to be angry?" Then Jonah went out of the city and sat down east of the city, and made a booth for himself there. He sat under it in the shade, waiting to see what would become of the city.

(Jonah 4:4-5)

Jonah is questioned by God about his anger, though there is no record of the prophet's reply. Dialogue has broken down. God's rebuke remains unanswered as Jonah leaves the city of Nineveh behind him, which is reminiscent of Jonah's silent flight following his first commission. Jonah does not head back home to Galilee, however, but sits in the shade, east of the city, waiting to see what will become of Nineveh. Even at this late stage, even after arguing with God and being questioned by God, he is still longing for Nineveh's destruction, still hoping for its annihilation, still dreaming that his outlook, not the Lord's, will hold sway. Jonah is hungry for apocalypse now. As Abraham witnessed the smouldering ruins of Sodom and Gomorrah, Jonah hopes to witness the same for Nineveh:

Then the LORD rained on Sodom and Gomorrah sulphur and fire from the LORD out of heaven; and he overthrew those cities, and all the Plain, and all the inhabitants of the cities, and what grew on the ground... Abraham went early in the morning to the place where he had stood before the LORD; and he looked down towards Sodom and Gomorrah and towards all the land of the Plain and saw the smoke of the land going up like the smoke of a furnace.

(Genesis 19:24-28)

Abraham's witness of God's destructive power is denied our prophet. Jonah builds a shelter for himself, probably made from branches and leaves, reminiscent of the booths the Israelites built after their escape from Egypt and during their desert wanderings. From inside the comfort of his shelter Jonah waits for the annihilation of the Assyrian capital. This seems strange given that the fate of the city has already been determined.

Perhaps Jonah is thinking: "If God can change his mind once, he can surely change it again. If God can be converted by the actions of the Ninevites, is there still reason to hope that he might be converted finally by the outlook of his prophet?" Or was Jonah hoping that the Ninevites' conversion would be short-lived, so that when they soon returned to their evil ways, God's wrath would surely consume them? Certainly God's judgement was not a guarantee of the city's future safety: was God's relenting merely a delay in final judgement? Whatever the reason, Jonah is willing to wait it out. The prophet's defiance, however, will end with his defeat.

The withered tree

The LORD God appointed a bush, and made it come up over Jonah, to give shade over his head, to save him from his discomfort; so Jonah was very happy about the bush. But when dawn came up the next day, God appointed a worm that attacked the bush, so that it withered. When the sun rose, God prepared a sultry east wind, and the sun beat down on the head of Jonah so that he was faint and asked that he might die. He said, "It is better for me to die than to live."

(Jonah 4:6-8)

Clearly God thinks that the shelter Jonah set up is no match for the harsh elements that threaten him: Jonah's construct is inadequate to his situation. The Lord, consistently kind as ever, saves his angry prophet from discomfort and has a tree grow up, its generous leaves affording him with shade. In some of the translations the tree is identified as a castor-oil plant, known, it has to be said, for aiding constipation. Whatever its botanical species, the tree's function is to provide cover for the prophet and give him respite from his misery. Jonah does feel better in the sanctuary of its shade. While God's kindness to Nineveh provokes Jonah's anger, God's kindness to Jonah awakens the prophet's joy. As the beneficiary of God's mercy Jonah's response of happiness is a new and surprising development in this story. Jonah is overjoyed; but his delight will be as short-lived as the tree.

Jonah by Michelangelo.

Rather than placing St Peter on the ceiling over the high altar of the Sistine Chapel, Michelangelo chose Jonah, as the prophet who prefigured Jesus. Jonah is the largest figure that Michelangelo painted in the Sistine Chapel. The muscular prophet lies back under the tree, his feet off the marble base. As Jonah's eyes appeal upwards to God, his right and left hands point to the city of Nineveh as he awaits its destruction. He is off balance. The great fish, on Jonah's left, has now grown small as a harmless memory.

With the arrival of dawn, another animal is instructed to play God's accomplice in the Jonah saga, this time a worm, drafted in to attack and destroy the tree. Overnight the worm fulfils its mission and, with the tree now withered, another accomplice is called for duty, this time the cutting east wind. Defenceless against this biting dust-laden sirocco, without shade and with the growing heat of the sun beating down on him, Jonah is totally exposed.

The scene of God's merciful concern is suddenly upended. God now withdraws his protection as creation joins its creator in a conspiracy against the stubborn prophet. Jonah experiences what it feels like for God's mercy to be revoked and strict justice executed – something Jonah demanded for the people of Nineveh. Jonah comes face to face with the large absence of God's mercy and the crippling effectiveness of God's justice. Would he wish to inflict the like on the Ninevites?

Sometimes, especially with those who have neither a sympathetic imagination nor an active empathy, people have to be forced to experience what they cannot envisage. They cannot go beyond the limits of their own world, encompassed as they are inside their private bubble. What haunts or hurts others is beyond the reach of their understanding; other people's fear and pain is beyond the range of their ingenuity to comprehend. They have to be made to feel this world, familiar to legions, that is alien to their grasp; they have to undergo what for them would be personal torment before they become wise to what others bear. God submits Jonah to this process in the hope that it might educate his heart.

Jonah undergoes personal torment: what he takes for granted, God's mercy and forbearance, have been suddenly withdrawn. Whether that will make him wise is another question.

Judgement has been passed on Jonah, not Nineveh. Feeling faint at the onslaught he is experiencing, afflicted by what is happening, Jonah does not turn to God and show any sign of changing his mind: again a new experience has not made him wiser or more sympathetic. His anger still intact, he consults only himself, expressing his wish to die. He does not, as he did formerly, make this request of God; Jonah now speaks to his own soul in a short soliloquy. He is now reduced to talking to himself. Better to die, Jonah reckons, than to live with the shame and disappointment he is experiencing. He has been outside the city, waiting for destruction, but the city of Nineveh is not going to be destroyed. Given that, Jonah wishes for his own destruction.

God's final challenge

But God said to Jonah, "Is it right for you to be angry about the bush?" And he said, "Yes, angry enough to die." Then the LORD said, "You are concerned about the bush, for which you did not labour and which you did not grow; it came into being in a night and perished in a night. And should I not be concerned about Nineveh, that great city, in which there are more than a hundred and twenty thousand persons who do not know their right hand from their left, and also many animals?"

(Jonah 4:9-11)

God moves from saving Jonah from discomfort to challenging him about his views. Jonah has to learn that God's sovereign ways are not his ways; that God is not tied to our fitful sense of justice, but free to act in surprising ways and, it has to be said, in ways that we would find agonising – like Jonah does. Jonah is not a cipher, but someone whose struggle to manage his own preferences against the will of God speaks to all of us. His struggle is our own.

While God's anger receded with the pagan Ninevites, God asks Jonah why his rising anger is about a bush – a useful bit of greenery. Jonah's answer is immediate and unambiguous: he is angry enough to die. Given the enormous choices before our prophet, his sympathy for plant life seems somewhat eccentric.

We the readers are now confronted with a paradox: while Jonah is disappointed that the city of Nineveh has not been destroyed, he feels sorry about a solitary tree and angry at its destruction. Our modern Jonah is sensitive about issues on ecology while he fails to have compassion for a city of foreigners. His sensitivity is not about a tree, of course, but about the comfort it afforded him.

God has the last word: he asks Jonah why he feels sorry for a tree which he neither planted nor nourished, but objects to God's forgiveness for the inhabitants of the great city, which will open them to new life. Genuine forgiveness moves away from fascination with past wrongdoing to offer a new future. True forgiveness is liberating, for the giver and the receiver. The final question: should God not feel sorry for the 120,000 people in the city of Nineveh, who are clearly not managing their own lives, to say nothing of the dumb animals? The animals are accorded the final mention, an assurance that they are part of God's creation and can never be discounted from the human story. An intriguing ending, given that Jonah has been saved from Sheol by a large fish.

With God's question, the story of Jonah comes to an end. But, of course, the story is unfinished – a dramatic vacuum, like Samuel Becket's wonderful play, *Waiting for Godot*, a drama dominated by a withered tree. In his review of this play, the theatre critic of the *Sunday Times*, might have been speaking of the book of Jonah: "Such dramatic progress as there is, is not towards a climax, but towards a perpetual postponement."[40]

The ending of the book of Jonah is postponed; its resolution lies beyond the scope of this narrative. As the story of Jonah opened *in medias res* – in the middle of things – so it ends in the middle of things. No settlement is worked out; no tidy ending negotiated; no reconciliation achieved. The principal players, God and Jonah, are still at odds; the drama is unfinished. It waits to be completed beyond the confines of this Old Testament chronicle.

God's question hovers over the story and, indeed, over the whole of life everywhere. It is interesting that God invites Jonah to have the last word, and us the readers. As Paul Murray has written:

> We are no longer simply spectators of the Jonah story, but active participants. Each one of us must now respond to the challenge of God's Word, and to the direct call for forgiveness. Here on the open page in front of us – in the utter silence after the question – we are being offered the surprising freedom and opportunity to write out for ourselves as it were, the final paragraph of the book of Jonah.[41]

---

[40] Harold Robson, *Sunday Times*, 7 August 1955.

[41] Paul Murray, *A Journey with Jonah: The Spirituality of Bewilderment* (Dublin: Columba, 2005), 57.

We are all questioned by God's insistent and abiding mercy: "And should I not be concerned about…?" God invites us to go beyond our prejudices and allow a larger perspective to hold. **"And should I not be concerned about…?"** We fill in the rest of the sentence, if we dare, naming our favourite enemies, the people we would surely reckon to be beyond the reach of mercy or understanding. We pause at the names, or the races, or the religions. Whoever. Can we allow God to be the kind of God he chooses to be, scandalising us with his mercy to *those* people?

Jonah's response and our response to God's question, what he might say and what we might say, is beyond the scope of this book. But the writer of the book of Jonah prompts us to involve ourselves in the drama. As André Lacocque and Pierre-Emmanuel Lacocque observe:

> The story of Jonah is not only a religious manifesto; it is also a psychological tableau of the human condition. Jonah is not just a Jew of Palestine called out of his anonymity by a commissioning Voice from Without. He is human, he is everyone… Jonah, *qua* human, exemplifies our call to task. He is also a paradigm of our resistance to God's election, for nothing is more repulsive to us than to be designated (elected, chosen) by the Outer Voice for a self-transcending task, when we would rather follow our inner voice and our biological dictates ("what feels good") for our self-satisfaction and our self-aggrandizement.[42]

---

[42] André Lacocque and Pierre-Emmanuel Lacocque, *Jonah, A Psycho-Religious Approach to the Prophet* (Columbia: University of South Carolina Press, 1990), 217.

The story of Jonah moves within when we realise that the prophet's struggle is not an alien one beyond the reach of our understanding or sympathy. While it is a strange narrative it is not so strange that it leaves us cold and disconnected from the story of the reluctant prophet. The issues that Jonah faces are those which challenge all of us throughout our lives. The story of Jonah writes large the effort we all face in growing into our true identity, in following the right roads that take us beyond the limits of our own concerns, and in allowing the way we look at each and the world to be influenced by the indiscriminate kindness of God's mercy.

God's indiscriminate mercy

All the characters in the book of Jonah change their outlook, all except Jonah, the single religious figure in the narrative. We are left to imagine what will become of him and how he will face himself, his God and his world. The writer of this remarkable story is not trying to foster the readers' disapproval of Jonah – why write the story? – but to engage us in wonder at the inclusive favour of God: Jonah, the Israelite prophet, is the necessary foil in the ongoing drama of God's outlandish mercy. Jonah is not the first bewildered casualty of God's otherness; certainly, he is not the last.

Thanks to Jonah we can be sure that neither geography nor race has anything to do with salvation; that our past sins do not preclude the offer of God's forgiveness; that God's ways are not our ways; that the mercy of God can touch the most unlikely people in such a way that might offend us to the core of our being. God's mercy, it has to be said, can scandalise us. That is why Jonah's sustained opposition to the all-merciful ways of God goes beyond the limits of his personal story, connecting his struggle with our own lives in the twenty-first century.

The book of Jonah heralds the Gospel and the message of Jesus:

> Be merciful, just as your Father is merciful. Do not judge, and you will not be judged; do not condemn, and you will not be condemned. Forgive, and you will be forgiven; give, and it will be given to you.
>
> (Luke 6:36-38)

By choosing to change, the book of Jonah assures us, we can rework our lives. Change is good news because it means that nothing is determined and nothing is fixed. God's mercy makes fatalism redundant. As long as there is life, everything can be reconsidered; and it is God's judgement, not ours, which has the final say. Above all there is the extravagant message that supports the force of Psalm 130:7 - *Copiosa apud eum redemptio*: "With him there is plentiful redemption" – the motto of the Redemptorists. Jonah was the first to believe this wholeheartedly of God but, paradoxically, disapproved when he witnessed God offering it to his people's enemies.

The story of Jonah is, deliberately incomplete. No other book in the Old or New Testament concludes with a question awaiting an answer. But it is not just a question; it is this question from God: "And should I not be concerned about…?" That insistent question lingers for all our days, with God's entreaty to be God, to be recognised as totally other, over against the minor prophet Jonah's insistence to be himself.

Following God's question, what happens to our anti-hero? We return to the three questions which I think help us interpret the Jonah story for our own lives:

→ His **identity:** Who will he be now?

→ His **direction:** Where will he go now?

→ His **outlook:** From now on, how will he look at life and other people?

What will Jonah do when he leaves the great city of Nineveh behind him and goes where he goes? What will he remember of his experience? What will he learn, if anything? How will he pray, if he does pray? Will he, one day, hope that the mercy that God extended to the Ninevites will, finally and fully, be extended to him? All these questions are, of course, unanswerable. Thus we have to finish the story ourselves, for the story returns within. The questions are not just Jonah's, they are ours.

Our identity: Who are we? How many competing selves do we have? Which is our real self – the one we once set out to be and still, in spite of everything, long to be? What needs to be repaired about ourselves? What have we lost? What focus do we need to regain?

Our direction: What is our purpose in life? Our driving force? What are we for? Given our vocation, do we have to rework some choices we are making? Is there anything that has to give in us? Is there something that has to die in us? Like Jonah, do we have to be redirected to our original call?

Our outlook: How do we need to mend the way we look at the world and other people, particularly those utterly foreign to us, respecting their right of access to our God, the one who is also theirs?

As disciples of the Lord, we can only finish this story in our own way as we struggle to keep our identity, our direction and our outlook consistent and on speaking terms. When we do that we will arrive at ourselves.

Finally, it might be worth noting that in the pages of the Gospel we learn from Jesus a peculiar but appealing truth – that anyone can be our teacher, however unlikely they might first appear. Think for a moment of who is presented to us in the Gospels as people we can learn from:

→ The cautious aristocrat Nicodemus who prefers the cover of darkness

→ The woman of Samaria who has experienced a small litany of partners

→ The mad demoniac who runs around naked, harming himself

→ The clever steward who fixes his future before the date of his dismissal

→ The younger son who abandons home and family and wastes his freedom

→   The brother who refuses to obey his father's request
     to work in the fields

→   The child lifted up by Jesus and offered to the apostles
     as a teacher

→   The apostles who abandon Jesus in the Garden
     of Gethsemane

→   The principal apostle, Peter, who denies Jesus three times

→   The condemned thief, the sole supporting voice at
     Jesus' death.

The list goes on and on, not only in the Gospels but in life. We learn not only from the strong and the faithful, but from the fragile and the flighty; not only from the committed and the devout, but from the crooked and the cracked. Anyone can be our teacher if we can draw out wisdom from their story and benefit from their struggle. If we are all made in the image of God, it is biography, however singular and strange, that offers the best insight into the beauty of the Creator.

In the book of Jonah we have witnessed one dramatic period in his biography. And, yes, Jonah is offered to us as an unusual teacher – awkward, reluctant, disobedient, opinionated, fearful, flighty; the one who remains stubborn to the end. We might be aghast at his nerve and defiance; we might be appalled at his longing for death in the midst of life; we might be sympathetic to his demanding mission and his loss of face; we might be shocked at his stubbornness to argue his case against the all-merciful God.

For all that, Jonah is given to us as our teacher. What can we learn?

The Book of Jonah

Jonah 1

Jonah tries to run away from God

1 Now the word of the LORD came to Jonah son of Amittai, saying, ²"Go at once to Nineveh, that great city, and cry out against it; for their wickedness has come up before me." ³But Jonah set out to flee to Tarshish from the presence of the LORD. He went down to Joppa and found a ship going to Tarshish; so he paid his fare and went on board, to go with them to Tarshish, away from the presence of the LORD.

⁴ But the LORD hurled a great wind upon the sea, and such a mighty storm came upon the sea that the ship threatened to break up. ⁵Then the mariners were afraid, and each cried to his god. They threw the cargo that was in the ship into the sea, to lighten it for them. Jonah, meanwhile, had gone down into the hold of the ship and had lain down, and was fast asleep. ⁶The captain came and said to him, "What are you doing sound asleep? Get up, call on your god! Perhaps the god will spare us a thought so that we do not perish."

⁷ The sailors said to one another, "Come, let us cast lots, so that we may know on whose account this calamity has come upon us." So they cast lots, and the lot fell on Jonah. ⁸Then they said to him, "Tell us why this calamity has come upon us. What is your occupation? Where do you come from? What is your country? And of what people are you?" ⁹"I am a Hebrew," he replied. "I worship the LORD, the God of heaven, who made the sea and the dry land." ¹⁰Then the men were even more afraid, and said to him, "What is this that you have done!" For the men knew that he was fleeing from the presence of the LORD, because he had told them so.

¹¹ Then they said to him, "What shall we do to you, that the sea may quieten down for us?" For the sea was growing more and more tempestuous. ¹²He said to them, "Pick me up and throw me into the sea; then the sea will quieten down for you; for I know it is because of me that this great storm has come upon you." ¹³Nevertheless, the men rowed hard to bring the ship back to land, but they could not, for the sea grew more and more stormy against them. ¹⁴Then they cried out to the LORD, "Please, O LORD, we pray, do not let us perish on account of this man's life. Do not make us guilty of innocent blood; for you, O LORD, have done as it pleased you." ¹⁵So they picked Jonah up and threw him into the sea; and the sea ceased from its raging. ¹⁶Then the men feared the LORD even more, and they offered a sacrifice to the LORD and made vows.

¹⁷ But the LORD provided a large fish to swallow up Jonah; and Jonah was in the belly of the fish for three days and three nights.

Jonah 2

A psalm of thanksgiving

2 Then Jonah prayed to the Lᴏʀᴅ his God from the belly of the fish,
²saying,
"I called to the Lᴏʀᴅ out of my distress,
  and he answered me;
out of the belly of Sheol I cried,
  and you heard my voice.
³ You cast me into the deep,
  into the heart of the seas,
  and the flood surrounded me;
all your waves and your billows
  passed over me.
⁴ Then I said, 'I am driven away
  from your sight;
how shall I look again
  upon your holy temple?'
⁵ The waters closed in over me;
  the deep surrounded me;
weeds were wrapped around my head
⁶ at the roots of the mountains.
I went down to the land
  whose bars closed upon me for ever;
yet you brought up my life from the Pit,
  O Lᴏʀᴅ my God.
⁷ As my life was ebbing away,
  I remembered the Lᴏʀᴅ;
and my prayer came to you,
  into your holy temple.
⁸ Those who worship vain idols
  forsake their true loyalty.

⁹ But I with the voice of thanksgiving
　　will sacrifice to you;
what I have vowed I will pay.
　　Deliverance belongs to the Lord!"
¹⁰Then the Lord spoke to the fish, and it spewed Jonah out upon the dry land.

Jonah 3

Conversion of Nineveh

3 The word of the Lord came to Jonah a second time, saying, ² "Get up, go to Nineveh, that great city, and proclaim to it the message that I tell you." ³So Jonah set out and went to Nineveh, according to the word of the Lord. Now Nineveh was an exceedingly large city, a three days' walk across. ⁴Jonah began to go into the city, going a day's walk. And he cried out, "Forty days more, and Nineveh shall be overthrown!" ⁵And the people of Nineveh believed God; they proclaimed a fast, and everyone, great and small, put on sackcloth.

⁶ When the news reached the king of Nineveh, he rose from his throne, removed his robe, covered himself with sackcloth, and sat in ashes.⁷Then he had a proclamation made in Nineveh: "By the decree of the king and his nobles: No human being or animal, no herd or flock, shall taste anything. They shall not feed, nor shall they drink water. ⁸Human beings and animals shall be covered with sackcloth, and they shall cry mightily to God. All shall turn from their evil ways and from the violence that is in their hands. ⁹Who knows? God may relent and change his mind; he may turn from his fierce anger, so that we do not perish."

¹⁰ When God saw what they did, how they turned from their evil ways, God changed his mind about the calamity that he had said he would bring upon them; and he did not do it.

Jonah 4

Jonah's anger

4 But this was very displeasing to Jonah, and he became angry. ²He prayed to the LORD and said, "O LORD! Is not this what I said while I was still in my own country? That is why I fled to Tarshish at the beginning; for I knew that you are a gracious God and merciful, slow to anger, and abounding in steadfast love, and ready to relent from punishing. ³And now, O LORD, please take my life from me, for it is better for me to die than to live." ⁴And the LORD said, "Is it right for you to be angry?" ⁵Then Jonah went out of the city and sat down east of the city, and made a booth for himself there. He sat under it in the shade, waiting to see what would become of the city.

⁶ The LORD God appointed a bush, and made it come up over Jonah, to give shade over his head, to save him from his discomfort; so Jonah was very happy about the bush. ⁷But when dawn came up the next day, God appointed a worm that attacked the bush, so that it withered. ⁸When the sun rose, God prepared a sultry east wind, and the sun beat down on the head of Jonah so that he was faint and asked that he might die. He said, "It is better for me to die than to live."

Jonah is reproved

⁹ But God said to Jonah, "Is it right for you to be angry about the bush?" And he said, "Yes, angry enough to die." ¹⁰Then the LORD said, "You are concerned about the bush, for which you did not labour and which you did not grow; it came into being in a night and perished in a night. ¹¹And should I not be concerned about Nineveh, that great city, in which there are more than a hundred and twenty thousand people who do not know their right hand from their left, and also many animals?"

Acknowledgements

The author would like to acknowledge the key role of Eliana Thompson, our creative designer at RP, in the production of this book and Jonathan Thompson for the cover illustration as well as introducing each of the five parts with his original Monotype Prints, offering his own imaginative take on the story of Jonah.